Beginning Progressive Web App Development

Creating a Native App Experience
on the Web

Dennis Sheppard

Apress®

Beginning Progressive Web App Development

Dennis Sheppard
Tinley Park, Illinois, USA

ISBN-13 (pbk): 978-1-4842-3089-3
https://doi.org/10.1007/978-1-4842-3090-9

ISBN-13 (electronic): 978-1-4842-3090-9

Library of Congress Control Number: 2017961107

Cover image designed by Freepik

Managing Director: Welmoed Spahr
Editorial Director: Todd Green
Acquisitions Editor: Joan Murray
Development Editor: Laura Berendson
Technical Reviewer: Phil Nash
Coordinating Editor: Jill Balzano
Copy Editor: Mary Behr
Compositor: SPi Global
Indexer: SPi Global
Artist: SPi Global

Distributed to the book trade worldwide by Springer Science+Business Media New York, 233 Spring Street, 6th Floor, New York, NY 10013. Phone 1-800-SPRINGER, fax (201) 348-4505, e-mail orders-ny@springer-sbm.com, or visit www.springeronline.com. Apress Media, LLC is a California LLC and the sole member (owner) is Springer Science + Business Media Finance Inc (SSBM Finance Inc). SSBM Finance Inc is a **Delaware** corporation.

For information on translations, please e-mail rights@apress.com, or visit www.apress.com/rights-permissions.

Apress titles may be purchased in bulk for academic, corporate, or promotional use. eBook versions and licenses are also available for most titles. For more information, reference our Print and eBook Bulk Sales web page at www.apress.com/bulk-sales.

Any source code or other supplementary material referenced by the author in this book is available to readers on GitHub via the book's product page, located at www.apress.com/9781484230893. For more detailed information, please visit www.apress.com/source-code.

Printed on acid-free paper

To true friends.

Table of Contents

About the Author

For the past several years, **Michael Wicherski** has been applying his business sense and acumen towards designing, developing, and implementing custom solutions for hundreds of Salesforce customers and has worked with clients of varying sizes—from startup "mom and pop" shops to Fortune 500 companies.

An avid progammer, and a nerd at heart, Michael is constantly searching for those bleeding-edge technological innovations which can squeeze that extra bit of efficiency into his work. He has collaborated on several published works as coauthor of *Learning Apex Programming*, technical editor for recent editions of *Salesforce for Dummies*, and as author of *Salesforce for Developers LiveLessons*. Michael is currently Director of Software Engineering at The Agency, a full-service, luxury real estate firm headquartered in Beverly Hills, CA, where he leads his team of developers toward revolutionizing real estate software.

About the Technical Reviewer

Haulson Wong is a Software Engineer who has developed on the Salesforce platform for 3+ years. He has worked with dozens of companies as a Salesforce consultant and has had success using the platform to solve common business problems. He is currently a Software Engineer at the Walt Disney Company maintaining and scaling large web applications in the cloud. On his off days he enjoys recording music, brewing expensive coffee, and working on his vintage motorcycle that will never run in a million years no matter how bad he wants it to.

Acknowledgments

Thank you to all my friends and family who continue to embrace, enhance, and enable the nerd in me on the quest of learning how to be more worthy of the nerd designation. To all my fellow nerds out there, we make the world go round—stay strong!

It would also be remiss of me to not mention the editorial staff at Apress, who have put up with my crazy schedule while getting this title to print, and my Technical Editor, Haulson Wong, who did an amazing job in making sure what I wrote made sense.

Introduction

Congratulations! If you are devoted enough to be reading this introduction, you will go far, since you clearly pay attention to detail. If you are skipping this introduction, and therefore are not reading this, congratulations all the same! You will go far because you want to get straight to the heart of the matter and figure things out by challenging yourself.

The idea for *Beginning Salesforce Developer*, and the rest of this series, came about from what I have observed in the current developer ecosystem for Salesforce. Although there are many who claim to be Salesforce developers, the truth is that only a handful of them truly understand the platform. *Beginning Salesforce Developer*, then, takes on the task of bridging the gap. It has been written specifically for two very distinct audiences: Salesforce administrators (and others) who have never seen code or written a line of code before, and developers for other languages and platforms looking to transition into being a Salesforce developer. Although the latter group may find certain sections in *Beginning Salesforce Developer* trivial, they are there to serve as a refresher all the same— they may help in *Salesforce Developer Pro*!

The layout of *Beginning Salesforce Developer* follows an approach of first introducing the basic concepts about Salesforce and the force.com platform and what each is. After the basic introductions are over, the reader will follow along to install and configure a developer environment which will allow them to progress through the remainder of the book. The remaining chapters will cover how data is structured and accessed, the two proprietary languages native to force.com (Visualforce and Apex), and how to create custom user interfaces and database actions on the force.com platform. *Beginning Salesforce Developer* also includes an extremely condensed version of Computer Programming 101 throughout the text where applicable for those entirely new to programming.

I am thrilled to offer you my knowledge and experience by putting pen to paper, and hope you will forgive my intermixed cheerful banter—it is something I had always wished the authors of my textbooks had done. Without futher ado, let us get to work!

CHAPTER 1

Introduction to Salesforce

Welcome to *Beginning Salesforce Developer*. If you have made the decision to pick up this book, carry it to the register, and fidget through your pocket for exact change, you may be one of the following types of people: a) a Salesforce administrator wanting to learn black magic development; b) a Salesforce developer looking to enhance your skillset and progress toward *Salesforce Developer Pro*; or c) someone who may or may not know what Salesforce is, or how to write code, but all your friends are talking about it so you want to find out what the hype is about. Of course, if you acquired your copy online, or in an otherwise "techy" (and hopefully legal) manner, you may also be one of the above.

Regardless of which type of curious cat you are, *Beginning Salesforce Developer* was written with all in mind. If you already know what Salesforce is, how it is licensed, and what the different instance types are, you can skip ahead to Chapter 2, but it might be prudent to brush up with a quick read of this chapter, just so we are all on the same page moving forward.

Note   The order of the chapters was laid out in such a manner as to progress in difficulty, and therefore is the recommended reading order. If you wish to venture off our beaten path and jump around, you do so at your own peril of confusion.

Salesforce and the Platform

First question: *What's for lunch?* OK, it's really: *What is Salesforce?* Salesforce, from a technical standpoint, is actually a product built on the force.com platform by a company called salesforce.com. Let's take another look at that since it's a bit confusing. Salesforce is the product; salesforce.com is the company; the underlying technology of Salesforce is a platform called the force.com platform. The force.com platform is a PaaS (Platform as

1

© Michael Wicherski 2017
M. Wicherski, *Beginning Salesforce Developer*, https://doi.org/10.1007/978-1-4842-3300-9_1

a Service) that is entirely Cloud based—this means that there is no physical hardware or software installation required by the user. A Cloud-based service also means that as long as you have access to the Internet, you have access to your service—there is no need for an IT person inhouse or expensive onsite hardware or for dealing with software updates and maintenance. You just pay the license and get on with your life and the Cloud has your back. "The Cloud," of course, is a synonym for "the Internet."

You might be saying "I've heard of SaaS (Software as a Service); how is this different?" Although they are similar, SaaS typically does not allow for much customization of the software you are using beyond user preferences, whereas PaaS essentially allows you to build your own software to expand on existing infrastructure. Since some of the offerings from salesforce.com are not customizable, but run on the force.com platform, you could refer to Salesforce as SaaS and the platform as PaaS. We'll be focusing on custom development of the force.com platform, so for our purposes, we'll be focusing on PaaS. You can read more about the force.com PaaS offering in the next section.

Now that you know what Salesforce is from a technical standpoint, let's take a look at what it does, and why so many people rave about it. Out of the box, Salesforce is a CRM (Customer Relationship Management) tool—in other words, it allows businesses to keep track of, and interact with, their customers. You can start with the simplest offering, which is essentially a glorified address book with some extra data and reminders, and progress through to the enterprise level, where you can have Salesforce autodial your next customer and pull up their proposal automatically for your sales rep. There really isn't much you cannot do on the platform: most of the limitations in place are through governor limits (covered in Chapter 5), most of which can be overcome in many ways.

Throughout this series, you will learn how to create custom applications and implement business logic tailored to your, and your company's, needs—built right on the force.com platform. The remainder of this chapter covers the under-the-hood details of the force.com platform as well as the different license and instance types you will encounter as a Salesforce developer.

PaaS and Multitenant Architecture

We have already covered what PaaS is, but what makes force.com so special? Part of the answer to that question is that force.com has a *multitenant architecture*. This means that there are hundreds, if not thousands, of companies all working alongside each other on the same servers, using the same common core of functionality, while still having all their data securely siloed and private.

There is always only one version of the platform that is in "production" (live) at any given time. Force.com achieves backward compatibility by segregating itself into tenant data, platform infrastructure, and *metadata* of the applications on the platform. *Metadata*, for the uninitiated, is simply "data about data." This segregation is what allows salesforce.com to release three new versions (releases) of the platform a year. salesforce.com promises backward compatibility so that these releases do not break anything, including all your apps and customizations.

Note   While the force.com platform is backward compatible, you will not be able to take advantage of new features within older customization unless it is updated to the most current version.

Warning   Every so often, updates within releases contain security patches/fixes/updates which may impact older customizations. In these scenarios, system administrators are provided ample warning along with guidelines on how to bring existing customization into compliance with the new requirements.

Salesforce Licensing

Over the years, salesforce.com has rebranded its license names and updated its offerings multiple times in response to feedback from the Salesforce community and through acquisitions or mergers. Although this has allowed new customers to have more straightforward licensing, it has left consultants and developers with a myriad of licenses to learn and navigate. Therefore, while it is important to know the generic categories and types of licenses, there isn't as much need for beginners to focus on their exact names.

Different License Types

Generally speaking, the licensing options provided by salesforce.com can be broken into two main categories: Salesforce CRM licenses and platform licenses. The main distinctions between these two categories are what comes included out of the box, pricing, and feature limits. The Salesforce CRM licenses include much more in the way of out-of-the-box objects (covered in Chapter 3) and functionality centered around them, generally have higher feature limits, and are significantly more expensive than

the platform licenses. Although the Salesforce CRM licenses are significantly more expensive, it is important to note that with the right team of developers and time investment, all of the functionality can be recreated using the platform licenses—after all, Salesforce CRM is built on the platform as well; this would, however, be a very large and expensive undertaking and it is not recommended.

Note   The two categories of Salesforce CRM and platform licensing are not a comprehensive breakdown of all licensing for other salesforce.com products and offerings such as Heroku, Pardot, or Desk.com which are beyond the scope of this series.

A comparison of the current Salesforce CRM and platform licenses and their costs is given in Table 1-1. The cost of the platform licenses may draw you in at first, but you should keep in mind that those are the most barebones licenses you can get and will have to build all functionality out yourself (which you'll learn how to do in subsequent chapters).

Table 1-1. *salesforce.com Salesforce CRM and force.com Platform Licenses[1]*

License	Tier (Edition)	Cost[2]	Apex Code Available
Salesforce IQ CRM	1: Starter	$25	No (none of the IQ tiers do)
Salesforce CRM Sales Cloud	2: Professional	$75	No
Salesforce CRM Sales Cloud	3: Enterprise	$150	Yes
Salesforce CRM Service Cloud	2: Professional	$75	No
Salesforce CRM Service Cloud	3: Enterprise	$150	Yes
Salesforce CRM Sales + Service Cloud	2: Professional	$100	No
Salesforce CRM Sales + Service Cloud	3: Enterprise	$150	Yes
Salesforce CRM Sales + Service Cloud	4: Unlimited	$325	Yes
force.com Platform App	1: Employee	$25	Yes
force.com Platform App	2: Apps Plus	$75	Yes
force.com Platform Admin	Admin	$50	Yes

---

[1]Not all license tiers (editions) included in table; license offering and pricing subject to change.

[2]Per user per month; current pricing at `www.salesforce.com/editions-pricing`

As you can see from Table 1-1, which is by no means a complete listing of all the different license types and "tiers" or *editions*, the list is rather long. The editions differ in feature limits, for example number of objects or tabs, the amount of data alotted per license, and things of that nature. The license types differ in what is offered with each license out of the box.

Note   Although feature sets are typically determined by license type, not tier, when transitioning from Professional to Enterprise tiers, there are a few additional features which are made available. Some of these features are also available in Professional for an additional fee.

Recently, the Salesforce CRM Contact Manager and Group editions (tiers) were changed to the "Salesforce IQ CRM" license type and tier(s). These are the absolute cheapest feature-filled (platform is barebones) licenses you can purchase, which allow for very basic contact management, but feature a strong integration with email inboxes. In fact, you can add on the Salesforce IQ CRM inbox functionality to any of the other license types for an additional fee.

Salesforce CRM Sales Cloud and Salesforce CRM Service Cloud licenses and tiers are the most popular "standard" licenses in use. The difference between Sales Cloud and Service Cloud licenses revolves around the out-of-the-box features specifically tailored for tracking sales opportunities vs. tracking support requests; otherwise they are very similar. If you have a business that both sells and supports a product extensively, including live chat, ticketing, or phone support, then the Salesforce CRM Sales + Service Cloud licenses are your best bang for buck for out-of-the-box functionality.

The force.com platform licenses are the absolute cheapest licenses which include the ability to write custom Apex code—the programmic language that Salesforce uses—you would need at least the Enterprise "tier" of Sales/Service Cloud licenses in order to have Apex code. As with the CRM licenses, the different "tiers" of force.com platform licenses differ in the specific numbers of limits which you will encounter, but the platform licenses come with the same features as an Enterprise tier CRM license. So you are looking at $25/user/month vs. $150/user/month to get access to basic functionality and the ability to build your own customization. Of course, that only gets you the lowest limits, so realistically for a small multiperson company you are looking at the Apps Plus tier platform license, which still comes in at half the cost of an Enterprise CRM at $75/user/month.

Warning   There is a small catch with purchasing force.com platform licenses only. It is required that you have an "admin" license. These licenses cost more than an Employee tier, but less than the Apps Plus tier. At the time of writing they are $50/user/month. You must have at least one of these licenses, which are restricted in use as administrative only to develop code and configure the organization's instance.

Instances and Organizations

The Salesforce ecosystem is broken down into what are known as *instances* or *organizations*. The two terms are interchangeable, and it is very commonplace to hear an instance referred to as an *org*. Every customer has its own instance that houses all of its users, customization, and data. Some customers may have multiple instances if they choose to segregate their departments, for example, or employ any other breakdown through which they wish to silo users or data within their companies.

Instance types can be broken down into three major categories: *Production*, *Sandbox*, and *Developer*. Production instances are the "live" instances which house all working data and facilitate day-to-day operations. Sandboxes are *configuration-only* clones of Production instances which allow administrators and developers to change settings and develop new functionality without affecting anything in Production; *configuration-only* means that Sandboxes will clone over all custom configuration and code, but not specific records or data. Once changes are tested and approved in a Sandbox, they get promoted to Production through a process called Deployment—more on this in Chapter 8. The final type is a Developer instance environment. Unlike Production instances, which can be linked to their sandboxes for deploying changes between each other, Developer instances are special, production-grade, and stand-alone environments provided free of charge to developers for the express purpose of developing customizations which will get packaged into apps for distribution on the Salesforce App Exchange, without the use of a Sandbox (you can develop custom code directly in the Developer instance).

Although there is only one type of Production instance, there are a few variations of Sandbox and Developer instances. The variations of Developer instances are beyond the scope of this series, and we will discuss the standard Developer instance type in the

next chapter. With regards to sandboxes, however, it is important for a developer to know the differences. Any Production instance which is capable of having custom Apex has access to, at a minimum, a Developer Sandbox. Recently, Developer Sandboxes have also been given to the Professional CRM tier—which does not have custom Apex code available—for the purposes of testing configuration changes. It is important to note, however, that these Professional Edition Sandboxes do not have the ability to deploy *Change Sets* (more on these later), and the customization must be manually redone in Production once tested and approved. Table 1-2 lays out the different Sandbox types and their relevant attributes.

Table 1-2. *Sandbox Instance Types*

Sandbox Type	Cost	Refresh Period	Data Allocation
Developer	Several included CRM Enterprise or above / with platform	24 hours	200 MB
Developer Pro	Varies, percentage of total license cost	24 hours	1GB
Partial Copy	Varies, percentage of total license cost / 1 included with CRM Enterprise or higher	5 Days	5GB
Full Copy	Varies, percentage of total license cost / 1 included CRM Unlimited or higher	29 Days	Same as production

Note   The Refresh Period of a Sandbox refers to how often you can clone over your Production metadata and configuration to the Sandbox. Be careful, however, as this process essentially deletes your Sandbox, erasing all of your data, and resets the Sandbox to a clean slate.

Although Sandboxes are only clones of configuration metadata (code and customizations), the Partial Copy and Full Copy Sandboxes also bring over some (partial) or all (full) of your data from Production. This allows for testing of new features with real data rather than testing data without affecting Production data, and therefore is excellent for testing.

Apex code development work (and really all changes) should first be completed in a sandbox, tested, approved, and then deployed into Production. This is the safest path to take to ensure there is no data loss and that your deployments remain smooth. If there is a Full Copy or even Partial Copy Sandbox available, a recommended structure would be to have a Development Sandbox as the development environment, which then gets deployed to the partial/full sandbox for UAT (User Acceptance Testing; wherein actual users log in and test), and finally deployed to Production.

You will always log in to a Sandbox instance at `https://test.salesforce.com`, and there is a visual cue to indicate that you are currently working in a Sandbox instance. This indicator is located in the top right of your screen where it says "Sandbox: " followed by the name of your sandbox (assigned when you create one)—see Figure 1-1.

Figure 1-1. *Visual indicator of user logged into a Sandbox instance named "full"*

In Chapter 2, we'll cover how to create a Sandbox as well as a Developer instance (where the remainder of the work for this series will be completed), as well as how to set up and configure the most common development software suites for development on the force.com platform.

Setting Up Your Development Environment

Now that the introductions are done, it is time to roll up your sleeves and prepare to get your hands dirty. You're going to need somewhere to do all your work, so let's sign up for one of those free Developer instances we discussed in Chapter 1. To sign up for a dev org (the shorthand name for a Developer instance), head on over to `https://developer.salesforce.com/signup` and fill out the following short form seen in Figure 2-1.

© Michael Wicherski 2017
M. Wicherski, *Beginning Salesforce Developer*, https://doi.org/10.1007/978-1-4842-3300-9_2

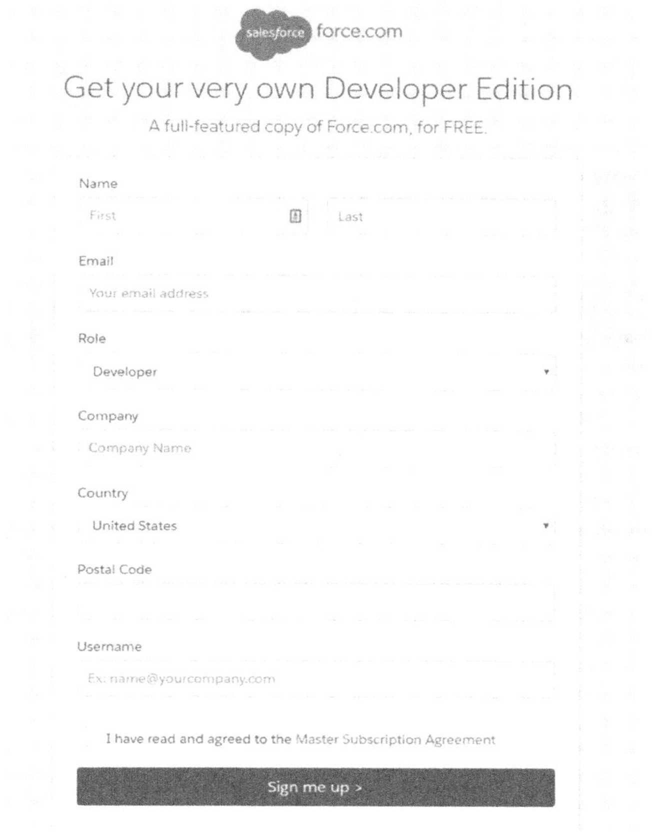

Figure 2-1. *Signing up for a Developer instance*

Note   Your username must be in the form of an email, but it does *not* have to be an actual email address. You can create something like mike@example.com and, assuming that username is not in use, you'll be fine. You still need a valid email address for the email field though.

You will receive a confirmation email with a link to verify your account and set up a password. Just follow the onscreen instructions to complete the process.

Tip   You will undoubtedly see many references to *Lightning*. This is the new development technology that salesforce.com has released and is currently promoting and working toward improving. Lightning will be introduced in Chapter 9, but for the majority of this book (and series), we will be focusing on Apex and Visualforce—the current and stable languages employed in most instances.

Navigating the UI

Once you sign up for your new dev org and log in and set your password using the link emailed to you, you should see the following standard UI (User Interface) view in Figure 2-2.

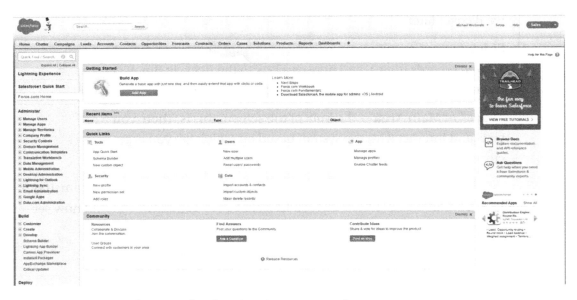

Figure 2-2. *Initial view after logging into a new dev org*

Tip   If you see something different, then somewhere on the top right of your screen you should see a link titled "Setup". If you still cannot see the following setup screen, you may have to click your name to open a drop-down menu exposing the "Setup" link.

This view, *Setup*, is where the majority of declarative (clicking) customization is performed by a Salesforce developer. Before we dive into customizing Salesforce, let's take a moment and look at the basics of interacting with Salesforce in case you aren't familiar with it already.

The standard interface is broken down into the following components:

1. **Universal Search** - this is used to search for any data across the entire instance.

2. **User Menu and App Selector** - used to access setup, user preferences, help and support, as well as changing "Apps" (Apps in the Salesforce context are groupings of tabs).

3. **Tabs** - controls which part of your instance you are currently interacting with. For example, if you are entering in a lead, you might be on the "Leads" tab. Custom tabs can also be created as we'll cover later.

4. **Sidebar** - a convenient place that lists helpful links, your recently viewed records (data), and houses a link to the Recycle Bin. It can be configured to house more useful sidebar components as well.

5. **"Page" / "Main Area"** - the bulk of the screen, this is where you view and interact with the system based on which tab you are currently viewing.

When you log in as a user, you will start on the "Home" tab—unless an administrator has configured your instance differently—so let's click over to that. You should now see what is in Figure 2-3.

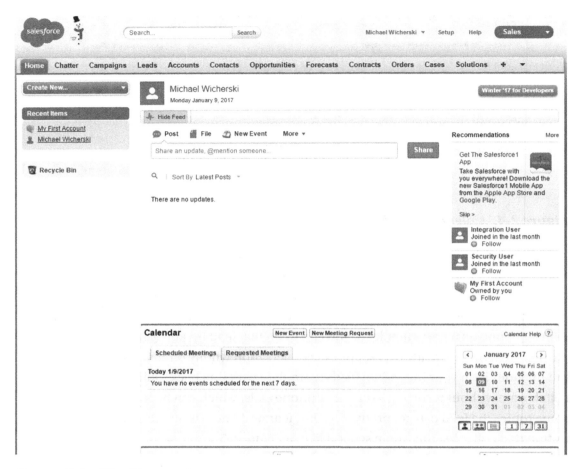

Figure 2-3. *The Home tab*

The Home tab is a special case for tabs in that it can be configured to display different things. Out of the box, however, it always contains the Calendar and "My Tasks" sections. These two sections go hand in hand to show you all of the *Tasks* which have been assigned to you along with their due dates, as well as any calendar Events you may have scheduled. Refer to Figure 2-4.

Calendar   New Event   New Meeting Request   Calendar Help ?

Scheduled Meetings   Requested Meetings   <   November 2016   >

Today 11/27/2016   Sun Mon Tue Wed Thu Fri Sat
                                                                                 30   31 01 02 03 04 05
You have no events scheduled for the next 7 days.   06   07 08 09 10 11 12
                                                                                 13   14 15 16 17 18 19
                                                                                 20   21 22 23 24 25 26
                                                                                 27   28 29 30 01 02 03

My Tasks   New   Overdue   ▼

                        You have no open tasks scheduled for this period.

Figure 2-4. *Calendar and My Tasks sections of Home tab*

Most standard pages, including the Home tab, will also include something called *Chatter*. Chatter is essentially a mashup of Twitter and Facebook for intranet use. Any user in your organization can @mention someone else, and you can do so on their profile page or feed, or you can do it on a specific record; for example, if you are working with someone on a particular lead, you can open that lead up and @mention your partner right on that lead. This keeps the conversation wholly on that particular lead, but includes it on your individual feeds (complete with link back), allowing you both to collaborate without resorting to email or phone calls, which can be lost or forgotten. On some topics the feed can get pretty long, but fear not! There is an included "Hide feed" button that collapses the whole section like in Figure 2-5.

Figure 2-5. *Chatter Feed*

Clicking over to a standard tab like "Leads", for example, brings up a perfect example of that out-of-the-box CRM functionality of the Sales Cloud CRM licenses we covered in Chapter 1. In Figure 2-6, you can see "Reports", "Summary", and "Tools" sections, all of which are CRM functionalities centered around the CRM "Lead". These sections link to reports you can run on your lead activity, launch tools to help you import leads, and other such functionalities available right from the get-go.

Figure 2-6. *Standard tab (Leads) view*

Figure 2-6 also presents standard features shared by all object tabs (objects are covered in the next chapter) such as the "Recent" view and *List View* selection drop-down, which allows you to select a filtered list of data to view. That's about as involved into the UI from a user's perspective as we will get for now. Additional functionality will be encountered and discussed as we progress through the chapters while discussing how to augment or replace existing functionality to tailor the instance to your needs.

Navigating the Setup UI

The UI in Salesforce for administrators and developers is much different than for regular users. Typically referred to as simply "Setup", the Setup UI does not make use of tabs, global search, the app selector, or the user sidebar. It has its own Setup-themed sidebar, and the interaction is limited between the sidebar and the main view area. Depending on how old your Production instance is (if you only have the dev org you just created, you have the most recent), the setup sidebar may not appear in the same order as it does in Figure 2-7. However, the options can still be found using the Setup search located in the Setup sidebar. Setup is broken into the following main categories, with our focus on build, deploy, and monitor:

1. **Administer** - this is where administrators manage security, users, and general access.

2. **Build** - both admins and developers use these options to customize the given instance to suit the needs of the business.

    a.   Customize - this is where you can customize standard features.

    b.   Create - this is where you create new items to build functionality around.

    c.   Develop - this is where you manage custom code such as Apex and Visualforce.

3. **Deploy** - developers use this section to perform deployments and manage Change Sets (see next section).

4. **Monitor** - both administrators and developers use this section to monitor the health of the instance, and developers can use these tools to debug issues which arise.

    a.   Jobs - ability to view and manage asynchronous processes which will be introduced in Chapter 10 and covered in more depth in the Salesforce Developer Pro title in this series.

    b.   Logs - used to define and view debug logs used in troubleshooting.

Figure 2-7. *Setup sidebar without "Monitor" section*

Setting Up a Sandbox

Once you are done learning how to write Apex, you will be working with production and sandbox environments rather than personal dev orgs. It is therefore important to know how to create a sandbox from a Production instance's setup area and link them together for Change Sets. Follow these steps to access the sandbox creation flow:

1. Click Setup

2. Navigate in the Setup sidebar under Deploy and click Sandboxes

3. You will now see Figure 2-8

Figure 2-8. *Sandbox creation screen 1*

4. Click "New Sandbox" to create a new sandbox

5. On the screen in Figure 2-9, you are asked what type of sandbox you would like and are shown how many of each type you have available. You also give your sandbox a name and description on this screen. The name should be short and descriptive; it is always best practice to include a description if the field is provided. Select "Developer" by clicking the appropriate "Next" button here.

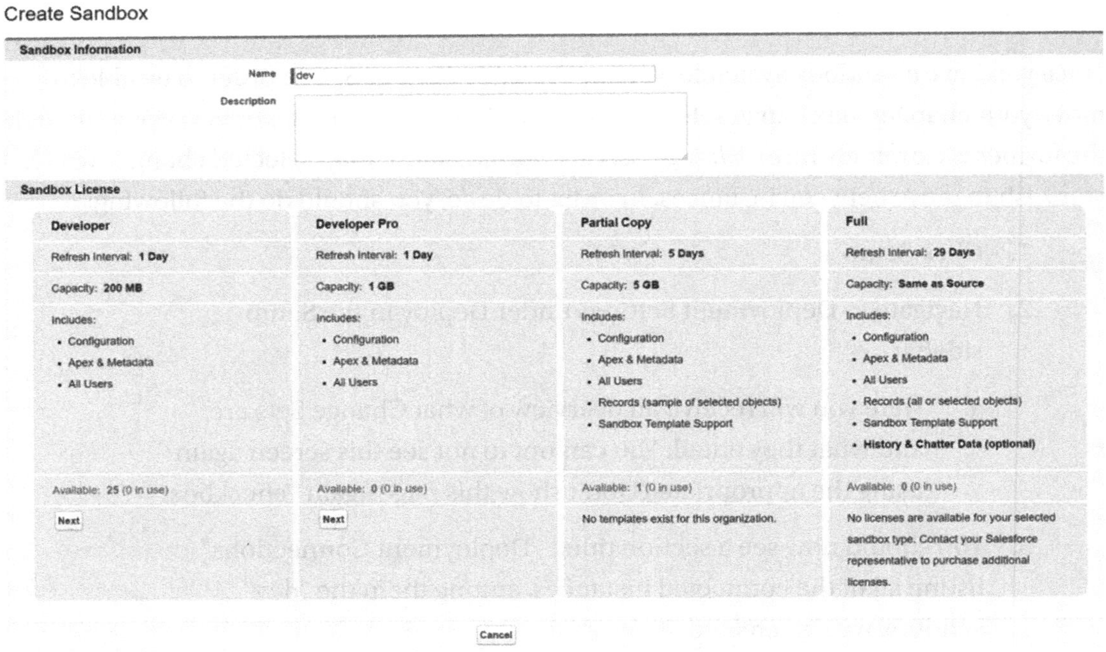

Create Sandbox

Sandbox Information

Name   dev

Description

Sandbox License

Developer	Developer Pro	Partial Copy	Full
Refresh Interval: **1 Day**	Refresh Interval: **1 Day**	Refresh Interval: **5 Days**	Refresh Interval: **29 Days**
Capacity: **200 MB**	Capacity: **1 GB**	Capacity: **5 GB**	Capacity: **Same as Source**
Includes:	Includes:	Includes:	Includes:
• Configuration	• Configuration	• Configuration	• Configuration
• Apex & Metadata	• Apex & Metadata	• Apex & Metadata	• Apex & Metadata
• All Users	• All Users	• All Users	• All Users
		• Records (sample of selected objects)	• Records (all or selected objects)
		• Sandbox Template Support	• Sandbox Template Support
			• **History & Chatter Data (optional)**
Available: **25** (0 in use)	Available: **0** (0 in use)	Available: **1** (0 in use)	Available: **0** (0 in use)
Next	Next	No templates exist for this organization.	No licenses are available for your selected sandbox type. Contact your Salesforce representative to purchase additional licenses.

Cancel

Figure 2-9. *Sandbox creation screen 2*

6. On the next screen it asks if you would like to execute apex after
    creation; leave this blank and continue.

Note   Your username for the Sandbox instance will be your production username
with the sandbox name appended; in this case, ".dev" will be appended to the
end of your production username. Your production password will also be your
sandbox password, but keep in mind that changing your password in production
after a sandbox has been created or refreshed will *not* automatically sync your new
password to the sandbox.

Sandboxes can take a while to create or refresh, depending on server load as well as
the size of your instance and how much data you are copying over, in the case of a partial
or full sandbox. Once your sandbox is ready, you will receive an email from Salesforce
informing you that it is ready.

Enabling Change Sets

Once you have a sandbox available, you must enable *Change Sets* in order to be able to move your changes via change sets from your sandbox to production or vice versa (though the former is extremely rare). *Change Sets* are nothing more than selected changes which you wish to move between instances. In order to do so, you should do the following:

1. Click Setup

2. Navigate to Deployment Settings under Deploy in the Setup sidebar

    a. Here you will receive an overview of what Change Sets are, and what they entail. You can opt to not see this screen again using the appropriate "Don't show this page again" checkbox.

3. You should now see a section titled "Deployment Connections" listing all of the connected instances, among them the "dev" sandbox we just created

4. Click "Edit" next to "dev" and select the "Allow Inbound Changes" checkbox and Save

5. Once the change saves, you can click "Back to deployment Settings" at the top of the page

6. You should now have a green arrow pointing from your "dev" sandbox to your Production instance as seen in Figure 2-10

Deployment Connections

A deployment connection allows customizations to be copied from one organization to another. This list shows the deployment connections allowed from other organizations to this organization, and from this organization to others.

This Organization: Wicherski Inc (Production)

Action	Name	Description	Type	Upload Authorization Direction
Edit	dev		Developer	Wicherski Inc ⟸ dev

Figure 2-10. *Change Set deployment connection enabled for "dev" to production*

7. You can repeat steps 1 through 6 in your sandbox to enable Change Sets from production to flow into the sandbox, at which point the arrow seen in Figure 2-10 would become double-ended to signify bidirectional movement

Once you have your sandbox and production environments connected this way, you can create Change Sets to move changes between your instances by navigating to "Outbound Change Sets" under the Deploy section of Setup. At this point, you would give your Change Set a name—preferably something descriptive of the changes being deployed—and a description. Once the Change Set is created, you will have the ability to add components (individual changes) by using the appropriate "Add" button seen in Figure 2-11. Once you are done adding components, click "Upload" and select the correct instance you wish to deploy to from the list. The Change Set will now upload and you will receive and email when it is ready to be deployed.

Change Set
Change Set test
« Back to List: Outbound Change Sets
A change set contains customizations to components such as apps, objects, reports or email templates. You can use change sets to move customizations from one organization to another.

After a change set has been uploaded, its components aren't refreshed and you can't add or remove components. To refresh the source of components and modify the component list, clone the change set.

Change Set Detail		Edit	Delete	Upload	Clone

Change Set Name   Change Set test
Description
Created By   Michael Wicherski, 11/28/2016 3:09 AM

Status   Open
Modified By   Michael Wicherski, 11/28/2016 3:09 AM

Edit Delete Upload Clone

Change Set Components   Add View/Add Dependencies

This change set contains no components

Add View/Add Dependencies

Profile Settings For Included Components   Add Profiles

This change set contains no profiles

Add Profiles

Figure 2-11. *Creating and adding components to Change Set named "Change Set test"*

Tip   Although you receive the email saying upload has completed successfully, it will take a few minutes for the Change Set to appear in your destination instance.

Note   You do not need to enable nor use Change Sets if you are deploying your changes by using an IDE (covered in the next section).

To see pending Change Sets in your destination instance, navigate to "Inbound Change Sets" under the "Deploy" section of your Setup sidebar. Under the section titled "Change Sets Awaiting Deployment" you will see a list of such Change Sets. You have the option to delete the pending Change Set from here, or you can click its name to bring you

to the detail page for that Change Set as seen in Figure 2-12. If you get an error message saying "Change Set Unavailable", just wait a few minutes; they take a while to become fully available in the destination instance.

Change Set Detail
Change Set test
‹ Back to List: Inbound Change Sets
This change set contains customizations that have been uploaded from a connected organization. If you aren't ready to deploy at this time, you can click Validate to preview deployment results without committing any changes. It isn't r deployment won't commit any changes if there are failures.

View Details		Validate Deploy Delete		
Change Set Name	Change Set test		Source Organization	dev
Description			Uploaded By	Michael Wicherski, 11/28/2016 3:20 AM
Expiration Date	5/26/2017			

Deployment History

This change set hasn't been deployed

Components

Action	Name	Parent Object	Type	API Name
View Source	WicherskInc		App	WicherskInc

Profile Settings For Included Components

This change set contains no profiles

Figure 2-12. *Inbound Change Set details*

From this details screen of the Inbound Change Set, you can choose to validate it (perform a mock deployment that verifies it can be installed without errors, but doesn't actually install it) or actually deploy it. Clicking either of the options will walk you through the next steps to complete the action; for most use cases, you can just hit next.

Development Environment Options

As a developer, sooner or later, you will come across the concept of an IDE (Integrated Development Environment). IDEs are applications that make a developer's life much easier by grouping together common tools and handling the "nitty gritty" of a programming languages so that the developer can focus on the logic rather than the setup. In the case of force.com, the available IDEs facilitate the connection(s) for downloading, compiling, and uploading changes to and from the force.com server(s). IDEs also tend to have helpful tools such as autocompletion and syntax checking (making sure what you wrote in a specific programming language can be understood by the computer trying to execute your program in that language).

Although there are many options to choose from with regards to an IDE for force. com, the next sections outline and compare the most common ones as well as walk you through how to set them up.

The Developer Console

The Developer Console is offered directly by force.com and requires no setup at all. It is accessed by clicking your name in the top right of the screen and then selecting "Developer Console". The Developer Console is a mixed bag of emotions for many developers; it is both a blessing and a curse. It can allow for very quick debugging, anonymous execution of short scripts, or quick simple queries, and it even allows you to develop custom code right inside of it. However, for large instances which are very busy (generate massive amounts of logs), or for developing on very large files, it can get pretty bogged down and slow. There is also the consideration that while you are writing code in the Developer Console, you are essentially filling out a web form, and if you lose Internet connectivity, you lose your work as you will be unable to save. It's also extremely easy to accidentally refresh the *dev console* (short name), causing you to lose your work. You can see the Developer Console in all its glory in Figure 2-13, and it is broken down as follows:

1. Logs - this is a running, live, list of all logs being generated by custom code being run by your user.

2. Test - used while running tests (covered in Chapter 8).

3. Checkpoints - allows specific lines of code to be monitored during debugging.

4. Query Editor - allows for quick execution of simple queries (more on queries in the next chapter).

5. View State - calculates the current view state of the page and shows what it's comprised of.

6. Progress and Problems - deal with deployment progress and any errors encountered during a compilation or deployment.

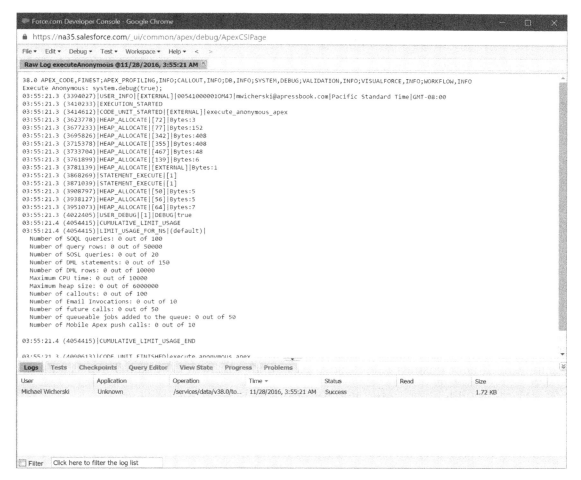

Figure 2-13. *The Developer Console*

The usefulness of, and how to use, many of these tools will become clearer as we progress through the series and get to use them.

IDEs

Although the Developer Console could meet all of our development needs, most developers prefer to have a robust suite of tools that also provide the ability to work offline and save files locally. This is especially true for larger organizations where there may be multiple developers and there is a *version control* tool in place (such as Git) which requires local files in order to operate properly. Version control is a tool which keeps track of revision history to files and who made them: you could think of it along

the lines of how Dropbox or Google Drive retain older versions of your files and allow you to restore them if you make a change you do not like or accidentally delete a file.

The most common IDEs for force.com development at the moment are MavensMate and Eclipse (or the Salesforce branded force.com IDE, which is really Eclipse). Both are cross-platform compatible (meaning they can run on Windows, Mac, and Linux), and each has its own strengths and weaknesses. If you consider yourself to be "very" beginner, the installation and configuration of MavensMate and Sublime may prove a bit challenging compared to Eclipse, but consider this a formal challenge to try to do it.

MavensMate with Sublime Text 3

In a very short span of time, MavensMate has become an extremely popular, if not the most popular, option for development on the force.com platform. It has many features, and can work with multiple text editing programs to leverage their functionality and turn them into true IDEs—most notably Sublime Text 3. It is currently being beta tested with Atom, and a version compatible with VisualStudio Code is in the works. That being said, since it is a third-party tool, it takes a bit more effort to install and configure than Eclipse, which is covered next.

To install MavensMate, first, you will need to install Sublime Text 3. You can download it (make sure to grab 3 not 2) from `www.sublimetext.com/`. There are no special considerations when installing Sublime Text, just install like any other application. Bear in mind that Sublime Text is paid software; if you intend to use it for actual work after you're done learning/evaluating it, please purchase a license key. Once installed, it is recommended to open the sidebar for open files by clicking View ➤ Sidebar ➤ Show Open Files. A successfully installed Sublime Text 3 should look like Figure 2-14.

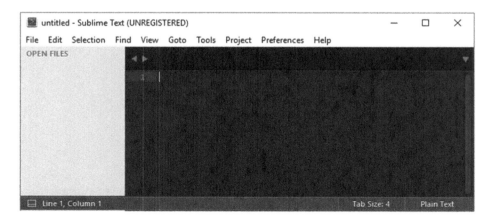

Figure 2-14. *Sublime Text 3 installed and open files sidebar activated*

Next, you will need to download and install MavensMate from `https://github.com/joeferraro/MavensMate-Desktop/releases`. The latest versions of MavensMate include a desktop installer, so just download the file appropriate for your operating system and it should take it from there. The developers behind MavensMate tend to release multiple "beta" version releases, but ask that people unwilling to be beta testers not download them. It is recommended to scroll down to the latest stable release when installing (v0.0.10 at the time of writing). Once MavensMate finishes installing, the confirmation dialog asks if you wish to start the MavensMate server. **Check this box to start the app.**

Warning   The MavensMate Server App must be running in order to use any of its connectivity features to force.com. If it is not running when Sublime Text is started and a force.com project is modified, you will receive a warning within Sublime Text to start this app.

The final step is to install the Sublime Text plug-in, which connects Sublime Text to the MavensMate server app you already installed. This is accomplished most easily by installing another Sublime Text plug-in called *Package Control* first. Instructions on how to do so (essentially copying and pasting a large blob of text) can be found at https://packagecontrol.io and clicking "Install Now". Copy and paste per the instructions and hit Enter or Return to run it. You should see some text scroll by. You should now able to click Tools ➤ Command Palette (or use the keyboard shortcut appropriate for your system), and type in "Install" and see the screen shown in Figure 2-15.

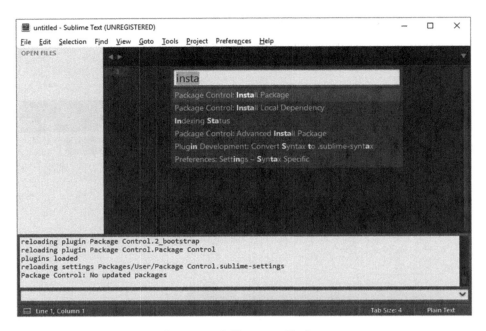

Figure 2-15. *Package control successfully installed*

With Package Control installed, you can use the "Package Control: Install Package" option from Figure 2-15 to search for "MavensMate" and select it to install. Once it finishes installing, you should close and reopen Sublime Text (quit on a Mac). You should now have a new menu option as seen in Figure 2-16 in Sublime Text called "MavensMate"; this is where all of your interaction between the two apps will happen.

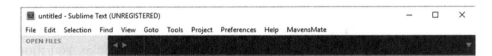

Figure 2-16. *Sublime Text menu bar including MavensMate*

Before we can download our dev org metadata into a local project for future development work, we must first specify a *workspace*. A workspace is simply a folder on your local computer where all projects and their files will be stored. In order to configure your workspace for MavensMate, click MavensMate ➤ Settings ➤ Global Settings. This will open the Settings page in the MavensMate app, and the first section is for defining a workspace. Depending on your operating system, follow the instructions on this page to pick a location. For an easy out, on Windows machines, you can simply use "C:\\My Workspace". Now let's get our dev org

27

metadata in here! Click MavensMate ➤ Project ➤ New Project. This will open the new project form in the MavensMate app as in Figure 2-17.

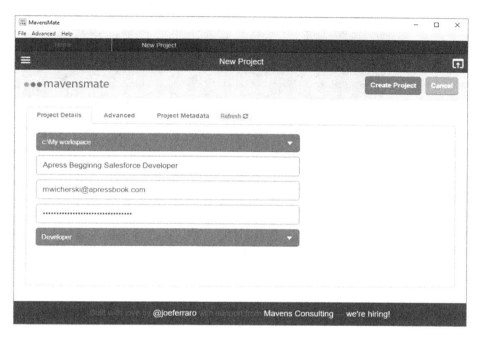

Figure 2-17. *Creating a new project in MavensMate*

The project name can be whatever you want it to be to distinguish instances apart. Your username and password are self-explanatory, but there is another piece of credential information missing on this form: the *Security Token*. The Security Token is used in conjunction with your username and password to access your instance from networks which are not included in your organization's security policies. You should always include a Security Token, if possible, in order to ensure you have access to your instance when you need it. In order to get a Security Token, log in to your dev org (login.salesforce.com) ➤ click your name ➤ My Settings ➤ Personal (in the left sidebar) ➤ Reset My Security Token. The token will be emailed to you and you should copy and paste it into the **password** field **after** your password - no spaces. The last option on this page, the instance type drop-down, should be set to the type of instance you are importing, in this case a Developer instance. Click "Create Project". The new project should be created for you automatically, and Sublime Text should pop back up displaying your new project as in Figure 2-18.

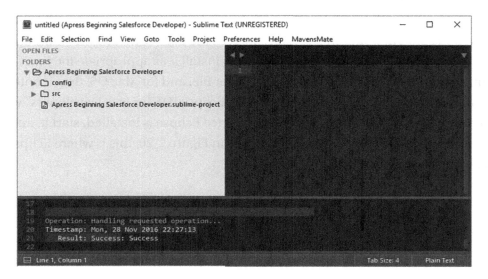

Figure 2-18. *Dev org project imported into MavensMate*

Tip   The latest beta versions of MavensMate use oAuth for authentication and no longer require security tokens.

We're now ready to venture forward and learn how to use MavensMate to develop on the force.com platform. It is recommended to also install and setup Eclipse, as certain points throughout the series will use it to demonstrate something, and it will be advantageous to you to be able to follow along.

Eclipse

Eclipse is one of the most widely used IDEs in the world and can support multiple programming languages. It is very robust and, like Sublime Text, has many plug-ins available. Eclipse can become a tool for developing on the force.com platform by installing the force.com IDE plug-in.

Tip   You may need to install a Java Runtime Environment if you do not have a recent version installed already. The Eclipse installer will prompt, and redirect, you to the appropriate places to do so.

To begin your installation, download the latest installer which is appropriate for your operating system from https://eclipse.org. At the time of writing, the most current version was "Neon". Once you download the file, install it as appropriate for your operating system: for Windows, open the installer file, and for Mac OS, drag it onto your Applications folder. You will want to install the "Eclipse IDE for Java Developers" version when prompted by the installer (Figure 2-19). Once Eclipse is installed, start it, and select a workspace directory when prompted as in Figure 2-20; this is where Eclipse will save all your project files.

Figure 2-19. *Installing Eclipse IDE for Java Developers*

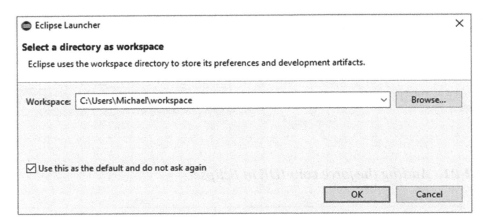

Figure 2-20. *Selecting a default workspace*

Tip   If you use a service such as Dropbox or Google Drive which stores versions of your files, and do not use or want to use version control systems such as Git, placing your workspace within your Dropbox or Google Drive functions as a makeshift version control.

After selecting a workspace directory, Eclipse will start up and present you with its interface. At this point, you can click "Help" and "Install New Software", which will bring up the installation window in Figure 2-21. On this screen, select the "Add" option, and create the entry for the force.com IDE repository by naming it "force.com IDE" and setting the location to the latest location found on https://developer.salesforce. com/page/Force.com_IDE_Installation (might be faster to Google "force.com IDE" - should be the first result). Click through the screens to install the IDE and then restart Eclipse when prompted (Figure 2-22).

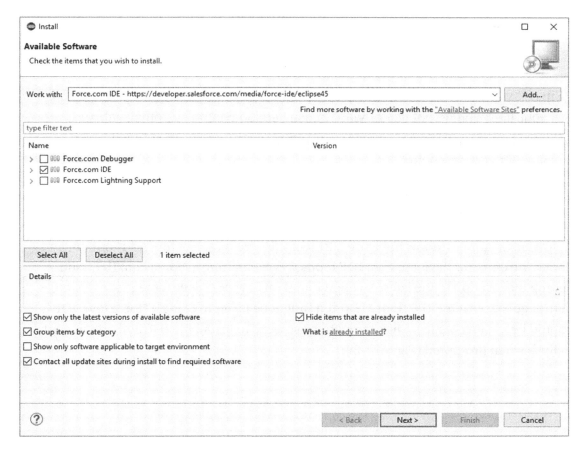

Figure 2-21. *Adding the force.com IDE in Eclipse*

Figure 2-22. *Installing the force.com IDE in Eclipse*

After all of the installation steps are completed, you should be back at the Eclipse interface. You can now select Window ➤ Perspective ➤ Open Perspective ➤ Other... and select "Force.com" from the list. You should take a moment to arrange your

workspace so that you feel comfortable with it. I would recommend moving the *Outline* panel over to the left with *Package Explorer* and shrinking this left sidebar to reclaim some screen real estate. Figure 2-23 depicts a vanilla configuration of Eclipse ready for force.com development.

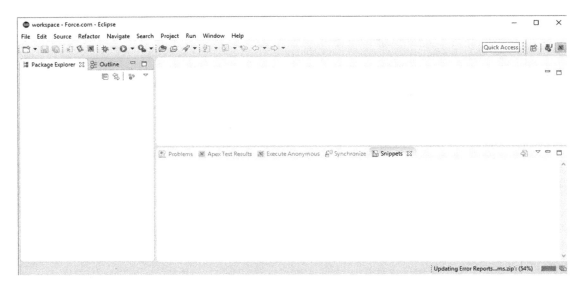

Figure 2-23. *Basic setup of Eclipse for force.com development*

The last thing left to do in order to start developing is to import your instance's metadata into an Eclipse project. You can do so by right-clicking anywhere in Package Explorer and then selecting New ➤ Force.com Project.

The first screen (Figure 2-24) that will come up will ask you for a project name, your credentials (username and password), a *Security Token* (these are used in conjunction with your username and password to access your instance from networks which are not included in your organization's security policies), and an environment (Production, Sandbox, or Developer). You should always include a security token, if possible, in order to ensure you have access to your instance when you need it. In order to get a security token, log in to your dev org (login.salesforce.com) ➤ click your name ➤ My Settings ➤ Personal (in the left sidebar) ➤ Reset My Security Token. The token will be emailed to you and you can copy and paste it into the appropriate field. The next screen, Figure 2-25, allows you to choose which metadata you want to sync over. For the majority of projects, you can just click "Finish" here.

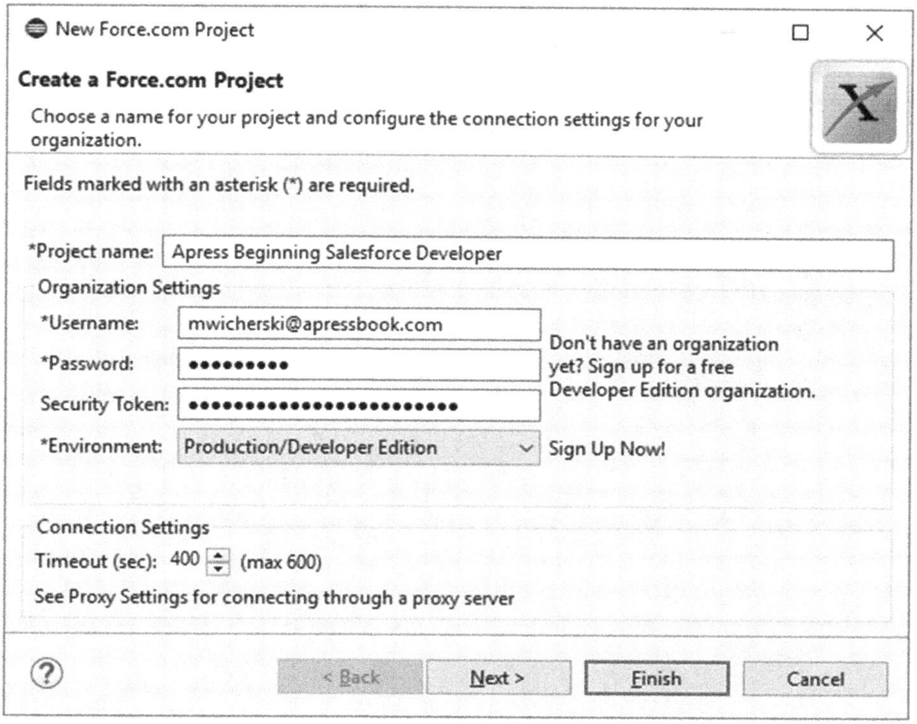

Figure 2-24. *Authenticating to an instance*

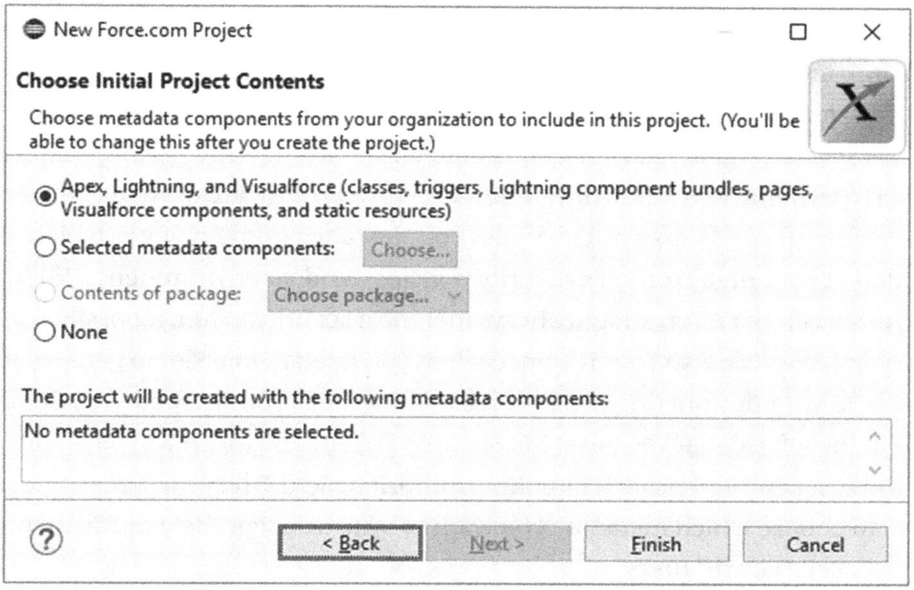

Figure 2-25. *Selecting metadata*

> **Tip**   When working with different types of instances in the same workspace (Production, Sandbox, Developer), it is always a good idea to differentiate the type in the project name. Common conventions are to use SB to indicate Sandbox instances, Prod for Production, and Dev for Developer.

You should now see your project in the Package Explorer sidebar panel along with a folder structure, which we'll explore in more detail shortly (Figure 2-26). For now, that is it; you are done setting up Eclipse for developing on the force.com platform.

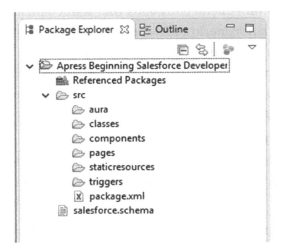

Figure 2-26. *Imported force.com project*

Bonus Setup Tips

The following are some additional plug-ins that I like to install in order to help optimize my development flow. These are completely optional.

Sublime Text 3

For Sublime Text 3 (which happens to be my editor of choice as well), I typically install the following plug-ins at a minimum:

Package control - allows for easy management of plug-ins; available at `https://packagecontrol.io/installation`.

SyncedSideBar - makes sure that the tabbed file you are viewing is also selected in the sidebar list of files and scrolled into view (helps with long lists).

Auto Semi-Colon - intelligently adds your semicolon to the end of the line in certain scenarios. For example, when you type "(" Sublime auto adds the closing parenthesis and puts your cursor in between them. When calling a function with no parameters, simply typing ";" will pop it at the end of the line, saving you a right arrow tap.

SublimeCodeIntel - adds a level of intelligence to the autocomplete functions to help suggest things you have already typed and predicts new suggestions based on metadata provided by the IDE

All Autocomplete - searches open tabs to help with autocomplete suggestions; great for when you have new variables to make sure naming and capitalization are consistent.

After installing package control, in order to get the other plug-ins, simply press the Ctrl+Shift+p combo (or Command+Shift+p on Mac) to bring up the package control interface. Then select "install package" and start typing the name, then select from list and it will take it from there.

Eclipse

For Eclipse, the only real suggestion other than switching to the Force.com perspective would be to add the *Snippets* view to your workspace. To do so, click Window ➤ Show View ➤ Other ➤ General ➤ Snippets and click "Ok". Snippets are a great time-saving tool that allows you to save commonly used blocks of code that you don't want to memorize or retype all the time and quickly insert them. In fact, I often use this feature to pull snippets of code that I then copy and paste into Sublime.

Chrome

I use Chrome as my daily driver, and I cannot imagine administrating or developing without the following two addons:

> **Salesforce.com Quick Login As** - by Kyle Peterson: there is just no faster way to figure out what the problem is that a user is facing than trying it out on their account. This allows you to quickly log in as the correct user without going through long lists of users.

> **Salesforce.com Enhanced Formula Editor** - by Kyle Peterson: this one is a bit more quirky, and sometimes I end up disabling it, but when writing complex formula fields (see Chapter 3), it is nice to have syntax highlighting and parenthesis matching inline.

Summary

Now that we have a Developer instance of Salesforce all set up and ready to go, along with our IDE(s) configured, we can dive into some real content. In the next chapter, we will take a look at how data is structured on the Force.com platform; a solid understanding of how the data is stored and related will be crucial in the later chapters when building out custom features.

CHAPTER 3

Structure of Data

Recall from Chapter 1 our discussion of metadata and how instances are all defined by it. In this chapter, we are going to elaborate on how all data is stored on force.com. In simplest terms, everything is an *object*, and has *records* specific to your instance. Table 3-1 can be used as a reference for terminology you may be more familiar with to represent the concepts of *objects*, *records*, and *fields*.

Table 3-1. *Comparison of Terminology Regarding Ddata*

force.com	Spreadsheet	SQL	Object-Oriented Programming
Object	Sheet	Table	Class / object
Field	Column	Column	Attribute
Record	Row	Row	Object / instance
Instance / org	File	Database	Execution instance

In the next sections, we will cover the database model employed by force.com, how to configure security for your data, how to generate data without code, and how to query that data using the Developer Console. In order to perform the queries, we will also cover force.com's query languages. Grab a good cup of coffee or tea as this chapter is mostly text, and readers should be comfortable with the majority of information covered before moving on to subsequent chapters.

Objects

Objects are essentially containers of fields. In other databases, they are commonly referred to as tables. In Excel, and other spreadsheet software, these would be your sheets. In the same way that you would name your sheet in Excel instead of leaving it as

© Michael Wicherski 2017
M. Wicherski, *Beginning Salesforce Developer*, https://doi.org/10.1007/978-1-4842-3300-9_3

"Sheet 1", objects must have a name and can have certain features turned on or off (e.g., the ability to log activities, run reports, and the like). Read on for an overview of some standard objects and fields.

Standard Platform

The first objects we will take a look at are those which are available for both force.com platform instances as well as the CRM licensed instances. These objects are therefore part of the standard platform offering. There are others—keep in mind that all the metadata about a specific instance is also stored in objects—but these are the most commonly used and customized ones:

- **Account** - this object is used to store information about a business account. Typically, this would be a business or firm. There are also use cases for using these as "household" containers to store multiple members of a family if you deal with families often.

- **Contact** - represents a person for whom you have contact information. This can be a contact at an Account (for example your contact person at a certain company), a household member, or a "private" contact (one which does not reference an account—more on this in fields).

- **Activity (Task / Event)** - Activities are used to store tasks (can have due dates, but do not have a time associated with them) and calendar events (which have start and end dates and times). These can be used to schedule follow-up reminders for yourself as well as meetings and are typically attached to the related record (for example a meeting with a specific Contact at an Account).

- **User** - the user object is used to store user records such as yours. This object contains information about your login information, personal information such as your first and last name, contact information such as phone and email, and other information that defines you as a user of the system, which includes your security access (covered later in this chapter).

- **Record Type** - although technically metadata, record types are records that are records that are attached to specific objects to create different "versions" of them. With an Account, you might have

"Vendor" and "Client" record types. The record types will allow you to filter and sort your data, but also allow the creation of page layouts (organization of fields on the object) specific to a record type; in turn, this allows for certain fields to show only for certain record types, and also for picklist values to be filtered for specific record types.

- **Others** - there are many other "configuration" objects with records stored which define your specific instance in the multitenant database on force.com. Objects falling under this category include the "Organization" object, which stores information about your instance such as number of licenses issued, API limits, storage limits, your instance ID, and so on.

Standard CRM

Recall that the Salesforce CRM (Sales and/or Service Clouds) are really just additional prepackaged objects and functionality on top of the force.com platform. In this section, we will take a look at the three most commonly used CRM objects (there are many, many more, but they all serve rather specific purposes that cater to specific business models):

- **Lead** - this is a very important Sales CRM object. It defines a person who could potentially become a Contact with an Account and an *Opportunity* for business with you. Leads can be thought of as your "clearing house." Every person you come into contact with should be entered here, and there is functionality provided to expose web forms for capturing leads on your website. When a Lead becomes "qualified" (you have done your due diligence and there really is potential for a business deal), you *convert* it. Converting a Lead uses a Sales Cloud feature to create an Account, Contact, and optionally an Opportunity from information on the Lead record. This process also marks the Lead as "converted" and it becomes uneditable, existing in the database only for reporting purposes. It now exists solely as a Contact.

- **Opportunity** - represents a potential business deal in the making. It has a status field which can be tied to a percent chance of closing field, both of which feed into a "pipeline" report allowing a quick view of all the potential earnings flowing into your company.

41

Opportunities are used to track the deal from inception through to closing, and can make use of **Opportunity Line Items,** which are links between the Opportunity and a **Product** in a **Pricebook** that has been preconfigured by an administrator.

Note   Opportunities and the related Opportunity Line Items, Products, Pricebooks, and Pricebook Entries are all Sales Cloud CRM objects. Before any user is able to use any of these other than Opportunities, an administrator must configure Pricebooks and Products, and then enter Products into Pricebooks using Pricebook Entries.

- **Case** - used to represent a customer-initiated contact attempt. This can be for support or just feedback. Cases have built in functionality to be created from a received email or a web form, or manually entered in by a user. The Case Comment object is used to create Case Comment records which automatically update the customer via email of a new response and allow for that customer to reply directly, creating a new comment. This is similar to how most ticketing systems work. The Service Cloud is heavily centered around this object, and most of the additional functionality you get from Service over Sales Cloud licenses focuses on Cases and optimizing user workflow around them.

Custom

The force.com platform is all about being extensible and customizable. At the heart of this idea is the necessary ability to create your own database for storing, manipulating, and retrieving data. Your limits in number of custom objects which can be created will differ by license, but the limit is high enough that it is rarely an issue.

Custom Objects are created and managed under the Create section in Setup, and their management is slightly different than Standard Objects. Unlike for Standard Objects, which break out different configuration into sections in the Setup sidebar, Custom Objects sport a detail page containing information about the given object, and this is where all the same sections can be found. We will see how to create Custom Objects when we begin building customizations in Chapters 4 and 5.

Custom Settings

Custom Settings are a special type of Custom Object. They count against the total number of Custom Objects allowed, and act exactly the same way as any other Custom Object, with the exception of one detail: they are always available globally without querying. If you are familiar with programming concepts, they are essentially global static variables; if not, then think of them as quick references, something along the lines of the clock on your computer: you don't have to do anything special to see the time, since it's always sitting in the corner for your reference. Due to their persistent nature, Custom Settings also have a smaller selection in the types of fields that can be added to them. These objects are typically used to store quick-reference data which should be visible and accessible by every user in the organization. Up until recently, they were a perfect solution to storing configuration data for custom-coded solutions so that administrators could change certain settings without having to ask a developer to recode something. *Custom Metadata* is starting to take over that functionality from Custom Settings.

Custom Metadata

Custom Metadata is actually metadata about metadata. It's confusing, but essentially, you are defining characteristics of data, which is stored as metadata that then configures the characteristics of your instance (data). What makes Custom Metadata significantly different from Custom Settings is that, as metadata, it moves around along with your metadata—think sandbox refreshes. If Custom Settings are being used to store configurations, then when you refresh a sandbox, you have to move that data over. Not so with Custom Metadata; it will just come happily along. There are still a few caveats to Custom Metadata when developing directly with Apex, but to make a long story short, if you are building an app that you plan to package and sell on the App Exchange (salesforce.com's app marketplace like the Google Play store or Apple App Store), then you should definitely be using Custom Metadata for configuration settings.

Fields

If objects are collections of fields, what are fields? Fields are most like *columns,* in other database systems as well as in Excel-like spreadsheet applications. These are columns like "First Name", "Quantity", or "Date" which define your data stored in the sheet in rows or *records.* There are a few standard fields that force.com puts on every

object; a few special field types that come included on standard objects and cannot have custom fields of that type created; and then there are custom fields which you can create.

Default and Special

There are certain fields which are on every object by default, and cannot be removed. There are also a few special fields which cannot be recreated as custom field types as of this time.

- **Name** – 80-character text field used to store the individual name of every record in the database; can also be set to be a formatted autonumber on Custom Objects.

- **Created By** - Compound User object lookup and Date/Time field present on every record in the database; comprised of CreatedById - User lookup and CreatedDate - Date/Time the record was created in UTC.

- **Currency** - Present on every object and must be set for every record if the Multicurrency feature is enabled in the given instance.[1] Stored in the database as CurrencyIsoCode.

- **Last Modified By** - similar to Created By. Compound User object lookup and Date/Time field present on every record in the database; comprised of LastModifiedById - User lookup and LastModifiedDate - Date/Time the record was last modified in UTC. If the record was just created, this time would be equal to CreatedDate.

- **Owner** - User object lookup field present on every record and object in the database except for those acting as the detail object in Master-Detail relationships.

- **Address** - standard compound field found on certain standard objects. Comprised of differing API (Application Programming Interface) names based on object, but always includes the following

---

[1]Multicurrency is a feature that allows organizations dealing with multiple currencies to keep track of currency amounts in the correct currency. Conversions for the purposes of reporting are done based on dated exchange rates.

components of an address: street, city, state, postal code, country, longitude, latitude, geocodeaccuracy. May also include data in countrycode and statecode fields if the State and Country/Territory picklists feature is enabled (fields are always there).[2]

- **Related To** - special field type found on the Activity standard object. Allows for a relational lookup to any object which allows Activities; stored in database as whoid (can only relate to the Lead and Contact standard objects) and whatid (relating to all other objects).

- **Geolocation** - special type of custom field which is a compound field using up three of the allowed total number of fields per object. Comprised of the geolocation field itself, the latitude portion, and longitude portion. The lat/long attributes are accessed by changing the suffix of the geolocation field API name. If the geolocation field is, say, home_location__c, the latitude would be home_location__latitude__s, and longitude would be home_location__longitude__s.

Calculated

Calculated fields do not appear on edit or data entry pages (as they cannot be edited), and are calculated on save of a record.

- **AutoNumber** - generates a formatted autonumber for every record created. When creating the autonumber field, you can set the format and select the starting number.

- **Formula** - special field type that allows for specifying a formula to evaluate the value, which can be conditional based, or a calculation. Formula fields have a number of different return types they can be created as:

  - *Checkbox* - the formula must evaluate to true or false

  - *Currency* - the formula must evaluate to a numerical value

  - *Date* - the formula must evaluate to a date value

---

[2]The State and Country/Territory picklists feature converts the country and state fields on address-type fields into picklists instead of text fields.

- *Date/Time* - the formula must evaluate to a Date/Time or date value

- *Number* - the formula must evaluate to a numerical value

- *Percent* - the formula must evaluate to a numerical value

- *Text* - here it gets interesting. A text return type for formulas can return any type of value (you may have to convert it to text using TEXT()). However, it can also return images and urls using the IMAGE() and URL() functions. A common use case for a text formula returning an image is to return a colored icon based on statuses, for example a green square for status = good and a red exclamation mark for status = bad.

- **Roll-Up Summary** - a roll-up summary only becomes available on the Master object in a master detail relationship. It allows you to quickly "roll up" data about the detail objects such as:

  - The sum of a certain field on all detail records

  - The count of detail records

  - The max value of a field across all detail records

  - The min value of a field across all detail records

  For all of the preceding, you can also specify conditions to only include records meeting certain criteria; for example, sum of total amount on all records where status = sold. Keep in mind, however, that there is a limit (currently) of 25 roll-up summary fields per master object, so use them wisely.

Tip   In Chapter 6, we'll take a look at how to create our own "roll-up"–like fields in case we need more.

Relational

Relational field types create relationships between objects. It often makes sense to group certain data together, without actually making it just one object with many fields. A great example of this would be a "Shopping Cart" object with related

"Shopping Cart Item" object records. You could then have a single shopping cart record that had multiple shopping cart items, each with its own data regarding quantity, when it was added, is it on a wishlist, its price, and so forth. There are three different types of relationship fields:

- **Lookup Relationship** - this is a "weak" link, meaning that you can leave it blank as far as the database is concerned. Your use case will determine whether you require this relationship filled out or not, and if any filters should be put in place to restrict which records can be chosen for the relationship—for example, excluding vendor record types from a customer lookup field.

- **Master Detail Relationship** - a "strong" link where you must fill this field in and there is no way around that. You can have up to a maximum of two master relationship fields per object, which turns the detail object into what is known as a Junction object. Junction objects serve the purpose of defining the relationship between two other objects. Taking our shopping cart example again, the shopping cart item object could have a master relationship to a shopping cart, and another to a product. Now, the shopping cart item defines the relationship between the shopping cart and the product by specifying quantity and any other attributes that are definitive of this junction. Master Detail relationships also provide an additional benefit over Lookups called Roll-up Summary fields. These roll-up fields allow for the creation of summary data fields which are based on the child object records, such as a count of child records or a sum of child record number field values.

Warning   Master detail relationships also have a very strong implication which needs to be considered during database design. Detail records in master detail relationships inherit their sharing and security settings from their master records. This means that if someone has access to the master record, they have access to the detail records as well. The detail record also does not have an Owner field; this is the only time that an object does not have an Owner field. *When a master record is deleted, all of its child records are cascade deleted as well.*

Note   Due to the implied sharing and security control of the master object in Master Detail relationships, standard objects can only be masters and never children (detail) objects.

- **External Lookup Relationship** - these are a way to link different Salesforce instances together or to include data in external databases. It is beyond the scope of this series, but know that you can define external data sources and then include their tables/objects in relationships with your Salesforce data.

Generic

The following generic fields are mostly self-explanatory, but some of them do have a few nuances to be aware of:

- **Checkbox** - represents a true/false value.

- **Currency** - represents an amount. Defaults to formatting consistent with the Locale setting of your user profile unless multicurrency is enabled. If multicurrency is enabled, it defaults to the Locale formatting of the currency selected as the currency for the record being viewed.

- **Date** - represents a date with no time aspect. Always stored in UTC and converted to the current user's locale setting when viewed. If utilized in a Date/Time aspect, defaults to midnight on the date set.

- **Date/Time** - represents a date with a specific time. Always stored in UTC and converted to current user's locale settings when viewed.

- **Email** - stores an email address and renders as a mailto: action URL in order to facilitate click-to-email.

- **Number** - stores a numeric value. Maximum digit length is 18, which can be split between whole numbers and decimal values; for example, 16 whole numbers and 2 decimals.

- **Percent** - stores a percentage as a whole number. When referencing these field types in code, you must divide by 100 to get the decimal percentage equivalent and multiply by 100 before setting the value.

- **Phone** - text field which gets formatted according to the locale of the user. Can input extensions by adding a space followed by an x followed by the extension number.

- **Picklist** - force.com's fancy word for a drop-down menu. A text field from the database perspective, the drop-down is rendered in the UI on display. Can now choose to enforce picklist values to only those defined as options.

- **Picklist (Multi-Select)** - a two-window list of options allowing users to move from left (unselected) to right (selected) panes. Stored in the database as a semicolon-delimited string.

Note   There is a feature called *Picklist Value Set* under the Create section of Setup which allows for the definition of values to be used by picklists. If you have a picklist that will be used multiple times, you can create and use these value sets when creating the picklist field. That way, when options change, updating the value set will automatically update the available options on all related picklists.

- **Text** - plain text field, maximum length of 255, defined when created.

- **Text Area** - plain text field which can support multiple lines; always 255 characters max.

- **Text Area (Long)** - plain text field with a maximum of 131,072 characters, which can span multiple lines.

- **Text Area (Rich)** - text area which renders with a rich text editor. Can support multiple lines and is stored in database as html-formatted text.

- **Text (Encrypted)** - special type of text field which can use masks to partially conceal certain data such as credit card information. Should be used to store any sensitive and critical data which not all users should see. Max length of 175 characters due to encryption. This field type also has a special permission centered around it to allow certain users to view the encrypted data while allowing others to only edit.

- **URL** - special type of text field that renders as a clickable link. Can omit the http in a URL, but must include https if desired.

Security and Validation

Being able to store your organization's data cleanly, and in an organized fashion, is very important. However, controlling who now has access to that data is equally as, if not more, important. This is a question that you should always ask yourself or an administrator for your instance: who should have access to this? There are many levels of access control on the platform. Since you are planning on writing code, we can skip the non-enterprise-level security nuances (they have less control). At the enterprise level, you can control security at the object level, record level, and down to a per-field level. You will also retain control over access to your custom-coded customizations.

Security

The Sharing Model is defined by starting at the organization level, Organization Wide Defaults (Org Wide Defaults), and selectively restricted/exposed after that.

- **Org Wide Defaults** - here, you will set whether an entire object is Private, Public Read-Only, or Public Read/Write. This will allow you to make all Accounts private for example, meaning that only the person who "owns" that record can see it.

- **Roles** - roles are used in a defined "Role Hierarchy." Roles in the role hierarchy should be created as "functional" rather than "real," meaning that administrative assistants should be placed above their bosses in the hierarchy. This may seem counterintuitive, but the way roles function with regard to sharing, people above you can see your data (if "Grant Access via Role Hierarchy" option is checked). By making the assistant above their boss in the hierarchy, you are ensuring that the assistant can see all of their boss's Accounts (which have been set to Private in Org Wide Defaults). Roles can also be used in *Sharing Rules.*

- **Public Groups** - used to group users together for the purposes of *Sharing Rules.*

- **Sharing Rules** - When an object is marked as anything other than Public Read/Write in the Org Wide Defaults, sharing rules can be used to expose records meeting certain criteria. For example, you could do something along the lines of "All Accounts owned by the Public Group 'Sales Team' should be shared with users in the Role 'Support Staff'". This ensures that when you request support, the support person can see exactly which record you are having trouble with, but other members of the Sales Team cannot see your Accounts.

- **Profiles** - the king of permission control. Profiles store an incredible amount of data regarding what users assigned to that Profile can do within the instance. This includes password policies, hours during which users can log in, locations from which they can log in, which objects and fields they can access (profiles can even override Org Wide Default sharing to give access to private records or deny access to an entire object—the sales profile members may not need access to objects specific to the Human Resources department, for example—even if those are set to Public Read). Profiles also control which custom-coded customizations are available to users assigned to them.

- **Permission Sets** - permission sets can be thought of as "miniprofiles," which are assigned to specific users. They have most of the same configuration options as profiles and are used to grant additional access to that which the profile gives. For example, you might have a profile that specifies that passwords expire every 90 days; you can use a permission set to assign "Password never expires" to specific users. Or if a profile doesn't grant access to a specific object/field, you can use a permission set to override that for certain users.

- **Field-Level Security** - can be set when a field is first being created; this access is stored on profiles, and can be edited there after creation. A field has the option of being visible (read) and/or editable. In order to be editable, the field must also be visible.

Tip Your first step upon receiving a bug report should always be to ensure that the user in question has access to everything they need in order to complete what they are trying to do.

Validation

As important as it is to have proper security, it is also important to have data validation in place, sometimes even to ensure that users are not bypassing security. There are three different types of standard validation in addition to custom-developed Apex code validation. Standard validation can be done through "Database" validation, "Layout"-based validation, and Validation Rules.

- **Database** – Database-level validation will always confirm that the correct type is being stored. For example, it will not allow you to store a value of 'twenty' in a field defined as a Number type. Database validation also comes into play if the "Required" checkbox was checked during field creation or "Unique" settings were set (case sensitive/insensitive). If records violating any of these validations are attempted to be inserted into the database, a fatal exception will be given and the data will not be saved.

- **Layout Based** - validation is added to the page layout when adding a field to the layout. This type of validation allows administrators to require fields be filled out for only certain Record Types that require them, while allowing them to be empty for other Record Types. Layout-based validation can also make fields read-only for users who would normally be able to edit that field.

- **Validation Rules** - formula-based rules which can be created by administrators to validate against business requirements. If these formulas evaluate to true, a validation error is displayed to the user with the specifying message.

Note   For users with the permission of "Modify all", layout-based read-only restrictions will not be enforced if field-level security allows them to edit the given field.

Creating and Retrieving Data in UI

Users will mainly be creating data by using the UI. There are some import tools available to them, but that functionality is typically something that administrators handle, and then there are customizations you are going to build to allow users to interact with the database. In order to know what will help users the most, you should always try to experience and understand what they currently use to address the need. To that end, let us walk through how a user would go about creating, editing, and viewing a new Account in our dev org.

Creating and Editing

The pages presented in the standard UI for both creating and editing records are the same exact page. When creating custom interfaces, you can override each individually, providing a separate page or even the standard page for either operation.

To create a new Account, click the Accounts tab and then the "New" button on the "Recent Accounts" section as seen in Figure 3-1.

Figure 3-1. *Account tab*

You should now see a form-looking screen with the standard Account fields displaying and editable. Notice the vertical red bar next to "Account Name". This indicates that this is a required field, and explained with a legend in the section header on the top right. As currently configured, this instance only requires a user to fill out the Account Name in order to save a new Account record. You'll also notice in Figure 3-2, some out-of-the-box functionality included with the platform to "Copy Billing Address to Shipping Address".

Figure 3-2. *Account creation/edit screen with required legend and copy address functionality*

Once you fill out your data and hit save, you will automatically be taken to the new record you just created, seen in Figure 3-3. Here you can see features such as the Chatter feed at the top and a *Related List* for Contacts. Related Lists are created when Relational-type fields such as Lookups and Master Details are created. In this scenario, a Relational field exists on Contact and points to Account. This is technically a Master Detail type field, but it is a unique one in that it is **not** required like other Master Detail fields, and you cannot use the Roll-up Summary formula, but Contacts still cascade delete when their parent Account is deleted and their sharing settings are inherited. This is part of the standard functionality, and is done so that "Private" Contacts can be created. If a Contact is created without an Account, then assuming default sharing settings, only you would be able to see it. This is great for keeping contacts such as your dog-sitter separate from company data if you want to keep everything centralized in Salesforce.

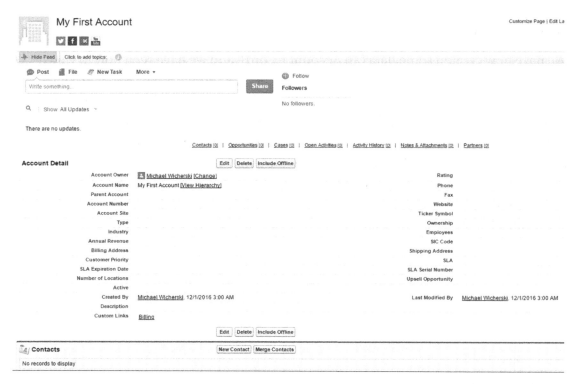

Figure 3-3. *Account view page with Chatter and Contact Related lists*

Related lists are also very handy because they allow you to quickly create related records. In this case, you can quickly create Contact records for this Account record simply by clicking "New Contact."

Tip   Clicking "Save" when creating a new record takes you to the view page for the newly created record. Clicking "Save and New" will take you to another edit page. You can continue this multiple times, with the final "Save" taking you to the view page for the final record you created.

Querying Data

We have now created some data (an Account record), and we have seen how to view details about that one record. Viewing multiple records at once is also possible. One way to do this is to use List Views (fancy name for a view that's a list), which can be filtered. To view List Views, simply click the tab for the object you wish to view records for. You can see a drop-down of available List Views toward the top of the view area, with a "Go!" button next to it (Figure 3-4). You can also create a new view by clicking the "Create New View" link or edit the existing one with "Edit". This would take you to a screen where you can adjust the filters and columns for the given view, but for now just click "Go!" This will show you a list of all Accounts created this week, "New This Week" (Figure 3-5).

Figure 3-4. *Selecting a List View*

Action	Account Name ↑	Account Site	Billing State/Province	Phone	Type	Account Owner Alias
Edit | Del | ⊕	Burlington Textiles Corp of America		NC	(336) 222-7000	Customer - Direct	MWich
Edit | Del | ⊕	Dickenson plc		KS	(785) 241-6200	Customer - Channel	MWich
Edit | Del | ⊕	Edge Communications		TX	(512) 757-6000	Customer - Direct	MWich
Edit | Del | ⊕	Express Logistics and Transport		OR	(503) 421-7800	Customer - Channel	MWich
Edit | Del | ⊕	GenePoint		CA	(650) 867-3450	Customer - Channel	MWich
Edit | Del | ⊕	Grand Hotels & Resorts Ltd		IL	(312) 596-1000	Customer - Direct	MWich
Edit | Del | ⊕	My First Account					MWich
Edit | Del | ⊕	Pyramid Construction Inc.			(014) 427-4427	Customer - Channel	MWich
Edit | Del | ⊕	sForce		CA	(415) 901-7000		MWich
Edit | Del | ⊕	United Oil & Gas Corp.		NY	(212) 842-5500	Customer - Direct	MWich
Edit | Del | ⊕	United Oil & Gas, Singapore		Singapore	(650) 450-8810	Customer - Direct	MWich
Edit | Del | ⊕	United Oil & Gas, UK		UK	+44 191 4956203	Customer - Direct	MWich
Edit | Del | ⊕	University of Arizona		AZ	(520) 773-9050	Customer - Direct	MWich

Figure 3-5. *List View of Account records new this week*

Another way to retrieve your stored data is to run Reports, but that's beyond the scope of this series, so we will just jump straight to the final way, which is to use database queries. A query, or a "question", can be issued to the database to retrieve data that matches your criteria. Such a query would be similar to: "Show me <specific data> from all <object records> where <my criteria>". In certain database systems, a query can also be used to create, modify, and delete tables and columns as well as insert, modify, and delete data. In Salesforce, queries are always read-only.

SOQL

The language used to query the Salesforce database is SOQL (Salesforce Object Query Language). SOQL should be used when the object and field for which you are querying are known. Otherwise, you should use SOSL (Salesforce Object Search Language), which is covered next. SOQL is used much more than SOSL in day-to-day development of customizations.

The syntax for SOQL is very similar to the English example used earlier: "Show me all <object records> where <my criteria>". In SOQL, this query to find our recently created Account record would look like this:

```
Select Id, Name, BillingState From Account where Name = 'My First Account'
```

In the preceding query, we are asking to receive back the Id, Name, and BillingState from all Account records where the Name of the Account is "My First Account" (when doing text-based filtering, keep case sensitivity in mind). Using the Developer Console (dev console for short), let's run this query and see our results.

To open the dev console, click your name in the top right of your screen and then Developer Console. Once open, click the "Query Editor" tab and enter in the query to the top box where it says "Enter SOQL or SOSL query:..." and click "Execute" as in Figure 3-6.

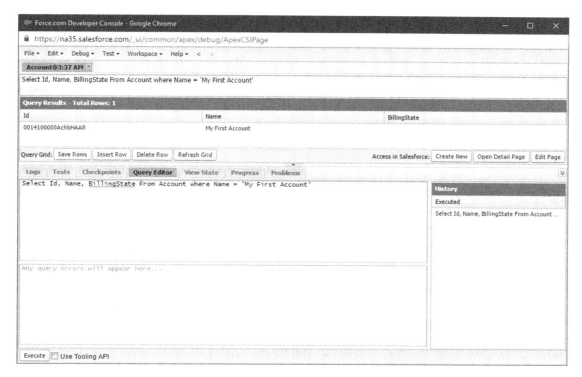

Figure 3-6. *Querying for an Account record*

You should see one result, matching the Account recently created. Unless you specified the Billing Address State Field (remember address field types are special), that column will be blank in the query return.

SOSL

Salesforce **O**bject **S**earch **L**anguage (SOSL) should be used mainly when you don't know which object or fields your results may be in. This is good for example if you know that there is someone in your database named John, but you can't remember his last name but know that it starts with Do. You could use SOSL to search against Leads and Contacts for records where the name field is like "John Do...." like this:

```
Find {John Do*} IN Name Fields Returning Lead(name, phone), contact(ID,
name, email)
```

This would search both Leads and Contacts for all records where the special field type "name" is searched for John Do* (* is a wildcard in SOSL meaning one or many characters; if you know it's only one character missing, you can use ? instead). If a record named John Doe is found in Leads or Contacts, it will be returned with the name and phone number if it is a Lead and with the ID, name, and email if it is a Contact. A record named Jane Doe would not be returned as a result of this query. Keep in mind that SOSL returns a list of lists of records; since you are querying against different objects it needs a way to distinguish resulting records by object type. This means that the response would be structured as a list containing a list of leads and a list of contacts. A good analogy here would be a sampler pack of chips—let's say Doritos. The box (SOSL return) contains multiple lists (containers) of different types of chips, one bag each of Nacho Cheese (Leads) and Cooler Ranch (Contacts) and each chip represents a record.

Tip   At the top of every page in Salesforce (with very few specific exceptions) there is a "search" box. This is known as the global search, which allows the user to search across all data in the instance. This is Salesforce's own implementation of a SOSL search.

Tips and Tricks

There are a few conventions in Salesforce around data that can make you look like a dark magician if you learn them (as if writing code wasn't enough sorcery).

Labels vs. API Names

When you create a new object or field (and certain other data throughout the instance), you will be asked for a minimum of two things: a label and an API name. A label is simply the readable version of what you are naming that will be shown to the users of the system. *API* stands for Application Program Interface, which makes the API name the name you use when you want to interface with the application as a developer. API names have certain restrictions to them. All custom objects/fields/etc. will have API names that end in __*c*. This indicates that they are custom. API names can be at most 40 characters long (37 to account for the __c) and cannot have special characters in them; all spaces, # signs, and so forth will be converted to an underscore (_). However, you cannot have two

consecutive underscores (__), as that is a reserved convention to denote a *namespace* (more on this later). When you type in a label and click out of the field, the platform will automatically generate an API name for you.

Tip Unless you have a very good reason for doing so, it is considered best practice to not alter the API name generated by the system. This allows other developers working with your data model to make the assumption that if they see a certain label, they can determine the API name without looking it up based on the conventions the platform uses to generate the API names.

For example, if you were to enter in the label of "Apartment Unit #" for a new field, the platform would generate "Apartment_Unit__c" as the API name. It is recommended to leave the generated API name alone, but sometimes there is already another field with that API name created; for example, there could be a checkbox field called "Apartment Unit?" which would have the same API name. At that point, it would be acceptable to change the unit # field API name to "Apartment_Unit_No__c".

Tip Do not include the __c in the API name field when creating a new field using the Setup UI. The UI will do this for you automatically, and it will also convert your __ into a single _ leaving you with a field API name of Apartment_Unit_c__c.

Querying Related Data

Another benefit of using Relational field types (Lookups/Master Details), is that we can then leverage the related data in our queries. For example, let's say we have a custom lookup field on a Contact with my name (Michael Wicherski) called "Secondary Account" that looks up to an Account record. If we wanted to find out what the name of that Account is, who the owner was, and what the billing state is, we could run the following single query:

```
Select ID, FirstName, LastName, Secondary_Account__r.Name, Secondary_
Account__r.Owner.Name, Secondary_Account__r.BillingState from Contact where
LastName = 'Wicherski'
```

The __r notation used in the query indicates that this is a custom lookup field (Secondary_Account__c), but I am not interested in the ID of the record that is related. Instead I want to traverse this custom relationship (__r) and get the specified field. You will notice that the exact same feature is being used to retrieve the owner's name, but because owner is a standard field, you do not include __r (there's no __c to start with!). If this is a bit confusing, do not worry, we will use it plenty in exercises throughout the series and it will become more familiar.

What's in an ID?

You have probably heard the phrase "What's in a name?" Although Shakespeare argued that there wasn't much in a name, there is a treasure trove of wealth of information in a Salesforce ID.

Length

The first clue is from the length of the ID. Salesforce IDs can be either 15 or 18 characters long. They both point to the exact same record, and you can use either while working within Salesforce; both will always work. The 15-character ID is the original concept, but it is case sensitive. When Salesforce started to be able to integrate with other systems, the need for a case-insensitive ID came about; this is where the 18-character ID comes from. The additional 3 characters are actually a *checksum*[3] of the capitalization of the first 15 and are typically used for integrations only despite functioning just fine everywhere.

Prefix

Every ID in Salesforce begins with the object prefix, which is the first three characters. As you become accustomed to working with Salesforce, you will be able to quickly glance at an ID and know exactly what object is being referenced (especially the standard objects which share a prefix across all instances). Custom objects have prefixes generated in an

---

[3]A checksum is a number derived from data for the purposes of error checking, or in this case, generating a unique ID since no other 15-character ID would have the exact same characters capitalized the same way (it is itself, unique).

incremental series based on the order the objects are created in. A few of the common prefixes to know are

00D - an instance ID

005 - User ID

001 - Account

003 - Contact

00Q - Lead

006 - Opportunity

00T - Task

00U - Event

500 - Case

012 - Record Type (though to access this, you need to go to Setup; knowing this prefix is just "cool")

Magic URL

The URLs in salesforce also give a ton of information away. For example, if you ever see "apex" in the URL, you know you are using a custom Visualforce page (covered in later chapters). You can also find out what server instance you are on (your entire organization is on this server and it rarely, if ever, will change). The subdomain before salesforce.com will tell you which server you are on as in Figure 3-7. This is also another way to determine if you are in Production or a Sandbox. Sandbox servers are always on "cs##" instances, whereas production, depending on where you are in the world, will be "na##", "ap##", or "eu" for North America (now Americas), Asia Pacific (now Asia), and Europe, respectively.

Figure 3-7. *URL giving away that this instance is on North American server 35*

Note   If your organization is using a custom domain, you will not see the specific server instance you are on. Instead you will see something like `customdomain.my.salesforce.com`.

If you are looking at a record, you can also see that record's ID in the URL. Going back to our "My First Account" record, you can see in Figure 3-8 that the ID is the same as that returned by the query (except for 15 characters in URL instead of 18 from query).

Figure 3-8. *Record ID in URL*

The final trick with URLs that will come in very handy in production is that sometimes custom interfaces (written in Visualforce and covered in later chapters) can't handle a data entry error. A good example of this would be when there was a data import performed and a field that should be filled out for a custom interface to work properly is not filled out. This should be addressed as a bug and the error handled, but that may take significant time while you have a user breathing down your neck unable to do their work. The solution in this case is to add a URL parameter of `nooverride=1` to the URL. This will return the functionality back to the standard view/edit page (depending on what URL you are attempting to view) and completely bypass the custom interface, allowing you to either correct the data problem so that the custom interface will work, or allow the user to work with the record temporarily.

Lovable Data Summary

In the business world, data makes the world go 'round. This chapter has thrown a huge amount of information at you, and it still only brushes the surface of all the intricacies of a good database design. Linus Torvalds (creator of Linux) once said that good developers care more about their data structures than their code. We are living in an age where new programming languages and new techniques for data analysis are cropping up daily.

The more data we store, the better—as long as it is good data. You can rewrite an entire application and use the same database if it is good. If your data model is horrible, you can spend as much time as you want on your application, but you will never be satisfied. This chapter is probably one of the most important ones in the series, as having a solid understanding of the data structures you will be working with, including the security model, will play a major role in determining how you approach your application designs moving forward.

CHAPTER 4

Introduction to Visualforce

Congratulations on setting up your developer environment. It is now finally time for us to get our hands on some code! The next step on our journey is to learn about the markup language that Salesforce.com uses for its different views and UIs. This markup language is called Visualforce, and it is very similar to HTML (Hyper Text Markup Language). If you have never heard of HTML or don't know how to write basic HTML, don't worry: we will be covering it in this chapter as a precursor to writing Visualforce.

Introducing MVC

MVC is short for **M**odel, **V**iew, **C**ontroller. Remember when you wanted to learn your first instrument, and your teacher would drone on and on about music theory instead of just showing you how to jam on day 1? Well, maybe that was just my experience with guitar, but this section is going to be entirely about software design theory and how force.com development aligns. Once we have that out of our way, I promise less droning.

The MVC software design pattern is essentially a way to break up various components of an application in order to make it clear what underlying technologies drive the application, and at which point. In MVC, there should be a clear distinction as to what constitutes your data model, how you can view that data, and what controls which data can be viewed or manipulates that data. Within the scope of the force.com platform, MVC is implemented with sObjects (Salesforce Objects) and their fields as the data model (as seen in Chapter 3), Visualforce as the view, and Apex controllers and extensions as the controllers (covered in the following chapters). All this really means is that in order to edit the data model, you should edit the objects and their fields; in order to edit the view, you should use Visualforce, and in order to edit control logic, you would use Apex.

© Michael Wicherski 2017
M. Wicherski, *Beginning Salesforce Developer*, https://doi.org/10.1007/978-1-4842-3300-9_4

Note   The model component of the MVC can also be customized through custom Apex classes defining objects. This will be covered in greater detail in the *Salesforce Developer Pro* title.

Bring On the HTML

HTML is the de facto language of the Internet. Every website you visit is using HTML to some extent to allow browsers to display the page to you. With a **markup language**, such as HTML, one can simply create a text file that uses **markup tags** to describe the content and structure of the document, such as a web page. When thinking about HTML documents, content is usually referred to as a collection of **elements** which are represented by tags, where an **element** is a specific portion of the document such as a heading or paragraph—even the entire document can be considered an element itself.

Using **markup tags** sounds fancy, but it is a concept you are probably already very familiar with, without even knowing it. When you write a document in Microsoft Word for example, and want to make something bold, you select the text you want to make bold and then apply the bold style. With markup tags, you would do the same thing, except instead of selecting the text, you would put a start and end tag. For example, to create some text saying "This is bold text" in HTML, you could use the standard tag for bold, which is **b**, like this: `<b>This is bold text</b>`.

All HTML tags are enclosed within <> to distinguish them from regular content, and the general syntax for tags is `<element_tag>content</element_tag>`. Notice also that the closing tag begins with a forward slash /. This is done to allow the nesting of elements while still allowing the developer to denote start and end locations of the various elements. Any tag can also be self-closing, and some elements are always self-closed such as line breaks, which represent a desire to move to the next line. These are written as : `<br/>`.

Tip   Although the HTML specification does not necessarily call for tags to be explicitly closed, it is best practice and Visualforce does enforce the closing of all tags.

Hello HTML

One of the most common and beloved traditions when learning a new language is to create a "Hello World!" example. In this case, let us change it up a bit and make it a "Hello HTML!" example instead. Putting aside force.com development for the moment, open up your text editor of choice (Sublime would be recommended). Once you have your editor open, type in the following code in Listing 4-1 and save your file with a .html file extension (helloHtml.html for example). Note the `<html>` opening and closing tags. Every html document must start and end with these tags, and because the entire document is wrapped into the html element tag, you can consider the entire document an element!

Listing 4-1. Hello HTML.html File Code

```
<html>
        <h1>Hello HTML!</h1>
        <h2>My name is Michael</h2>
        <h3>HTML is awesome!</h3>
        <p>This is a paragraph element</p>
        <b>This is bold text</b><i>This is italic text</i>
        <u>This is underlined text</u><br/>
        This is text on a new line<br/><br/>
        Two             lines                   lower
</html>
```

Once you save your file, you will notice that Sublime now recognizes it as an HTML file, and has *syntax highlighted* it for you according to language specifications for HTML. **Syntax highlighting** is a feature of IDEs that allows developers to quickly review their code. It works on the premise that different elements of code have differing levels of importance or invoke different functionality and are therefore displayed using different colors and sometimes even font styles. You can see this highlighting done in Figure 4-1, as well as Sublime indicating where the corresponding opening html tag is to the closing html tag the cursor is on (by underlining both). Once you open your newly saved file with your browser, by trying to open it like any other file, you should see something like Figure 4-2.

```
1    <html>
2        <h1>Hello HTML!</h1>
3        <h2>My name is Michael</h2>
4        <h3>HTML is awesome!</h3>
5        <p>This is a paragraph element</p>
6        <b>This is bold text</b><i>This is italic text</i><u>This is underlined text</u><br/>
7        This is text on a new line<br/><br/>
8        Two           lines                  lower
9    </html>
```

Figure 4-1. *Syntax highlighting*

Note   In the print version of this book, the syntax highlighting may not be apparent. The element tags have changed color to be orange.

Figure 4-2. *Hello HTML as rendered by the browser*

There are a couple of things to note regarding some of the HTML elements used here. You will notice that although our code has multiple spaces in the line Two   lines   lower, it rendered with only a single space in between the words. This is because HTML treats all consecutive **whitespace**, which includes spaces, tabs, and line breaks (enter key), as a single blank space. This allows a developer to neatly organize their code without affecting the final rendered display. Next,

you will notice that our paragraph element (p) automatically added a new line after itself so that our bold, italics, and underlined text all appeared under it, but the bold, italics, and underlined elements did not. This is a special feature of the paragraph element, as well as the heading elements (h1, h2, h3), and certain other elements. This is important to remember when nesting these elements, as they will always apply a new line and this may not be the desired outcome when displayed.

Tip   In the latest versions of HTML, using the bold (b), italics (i), and underline (u) element tags is discouraged in favor of using CSS (Cascading Style Sheets) styles. Although an advanced understanding of CSS is not necessary for Visualforce development, it would be beneficial for readers to familiarize themselves with the basics of this styling language—a very basic overview is included later in this chapter.

HTML Attributes

Arguably, **attributes** are where HTML's true power comes from. Although you don't necessarily have to use attributes when writing HTML to lay out your document, you will be hard-pressed to make it look good or control what happens with your content once it loads without them. You would essentially end up with a black and white text page with alignment, bold, italics, and underlined text. So, what are **attributes**? And how does one use them? Attributes are usually name=value pairs that can be added to any element's tag, specifically in the opening tag. Attributes allow the developer to specify additional information which describes the element. Some attributes trigger built-in functionality, while others allow you to store data for later reference. Let's look at a quick example. The **a** tag, for an anchor, is how you would create a link to take you somewhere; assuming I wanted to go to Google's homepage, for example, I would create the following element: `<a` **href**`=http://google.com>Take me to Google!</a>.` The "href" (hypertext reference) attribute here specifies additional information to the browser about this tag, specifically where it should redirect you when it is clicked. If the attribute were omitted like so: `<a>Take me to Google!</a>`, the link would appear as a link but would do nothing when clicked. If you look at the a tag missing the href, you should also be asking yourself "well, how does it know I want to go to google.com?"; really, any time you look at an element, you should ask yourself if it is missing something that would describe it and if it is, add an attribute.

Among the most important attributes to know are the **ID**, **class**, and **style** attributes. With these three attributes (and some very basic CSS and/or JavaScript), a developer can really control the layout and style elements, and even target the elements for advanced functionality. For example, an element's value can be bolded by simply adding an attribute called **style** with the value of font-weight:bold. Let's say you wanted to make a paragraph with bold red text: `<p style="font-weight:bold; font-color:red;>Bolded Red Text</p>`. Notice the semicolon after each style name:value pair. By using a semicolon, you can split style attribute values to pass in multiple styling changes. Let's add the Google link and our red text to our existing page as in Listing 4-2 and then take a look at what it looks like in Figure 4-3.

Listing 4-2. Updated helloHTML.html

```
<html>
        <h1>Hello HTML!</h1>
        <h2>My name is Michael</h2>
        <h3>HTML is awesome!</h3>
        <p>This is a paragraph element</p>
        <b>This is bold text</b><i>This is italic text</i><u>This is
        underlined text</u><br/>
        This is text on a new line<br/><br/>
        Two          lines                 lower
        <br/><br/>
        <a href="http://google.com">Take me to Google!</a>
        <p style="font-weight:bold; color:red">
                Bolded Red Text
        </p>
</html>
```

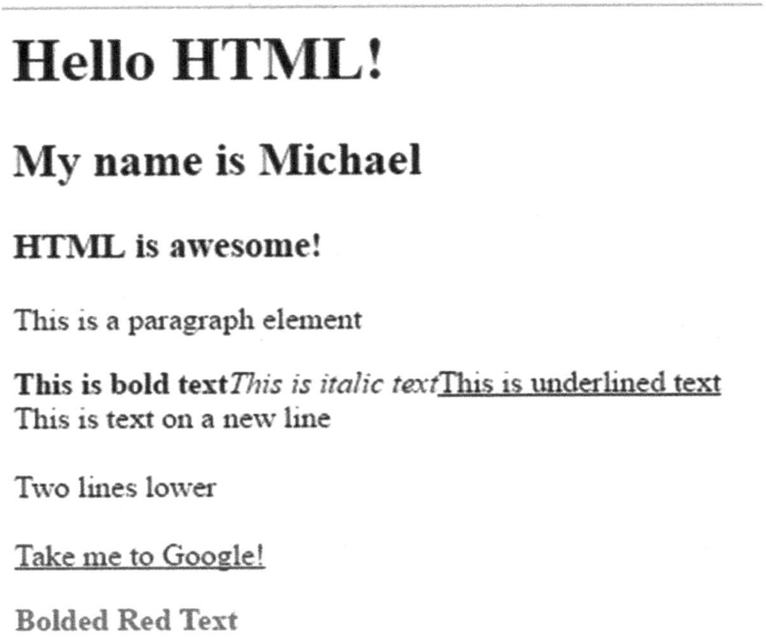

Hello HTML!

My name is Michael

HTML is awesome!

This is a paragraph element

This is bold text*This is italic text*<u>This is underlined text</u>
This is text on a new line

Two lines lower

<u>Take me to Google!</u>

Bolded Red Text

Figure 4-3. *Updated helloHTML.html file rendered with bold red text and link*

Note   If your link is a different color, for example purple, it is OK. Many browsers will mark a link a different color if you have "visited," or been to, the site already.

Tip   There are a multitude of standard attributes for HTML elements which vary from element to element. Luckily, you can easily find attributes for a given element by searching online for the specific element tag you are working with.

A Quick Primer on CSS

The **C**ascading **S**tyle **S**heets (CSS) language is the subject of many a pun among web developers. When you start building page layouts that need to be responsive (adapt to the size of the screen), or even when you just want to center an element on the page, CSS can become a real nightmare. Although a Salesforce developer does not really need to know CSS, having a basic understanding will definitely help; therefore, welcome to this section.

We have already used some CSS, specifically **inline CSS**, in this chapter in the previous section to style text using the style attribute of html elements. Now imagine if you had many paragraphs, or even just multiple lines of text, on your page that you would like to be bold and red. Typing out `style="font-weight:bold; color:red"` a couple dozen times would become very tedious, not to mention incredibly difficult to maintain if you ever decided you wanted the text to be blue and italic instead. In addition to **inline CSS**, which is so called because it is *inline* with the code, CSS allows for **embedded** and **external** style definitions. Embedded and external CSS differ only in where the styles are defined. In embedded, the styles are embedded within the same html document; in external, they are defined in an external file that is then imported. This brings us to the class attribute of HTML elements, which allows the use of embedded styles.

The class attribute allows the developer to specify one or several CSS style classes to apply styling to the element. Think of a CSS style class as simply a wrapper for your desired styling. As an example, let us create a class for our bold red font in Listing 4-3.

Listing 4-3. Bold Red Font Style Class

```
.myClass{
        font-weight:bold;
        color:red;
}
```

Now, to use this class on our paragraph from the previous section, we would change from `<p style="font-weight:bold; color:red;">Bolded Red Text</p>` to `<p class="myClass">Bolded Red Text</p>`. We can also make our existing bold text in the `<b>` tag red by adding the class there: `<b class="myClass">This is bold text</b>` to make our updated page code look like Listing 4-4.

Listing 4-4. Updated helloHTML.html Page Code with CSS Classes

```
<html>
        <style>
                .myClass {
                        font-weight: bold;
                        color: red;
                }
```

```
        </style>
        <h1>Hello HTML!</h1>
        <h2>My name is Michael</h2>
        <h3>HTML is awesome!</h3>
        <p>This is a paragraph element</p>
        <b class="myClass">This is bold text</b>
         <i>This is italic text</i><u>This is underlined text</u><br/>
        This is text on a new line<br/><br/>
        Two            lines                lower
        <br/><br/>
        <a href="http://google.com">Take me to Google!</a>
        <p class="myClass">
                Bolded Red Text
        </p>
</html>
```

Notice that the myClass definition is within a **<style>** tag at the top of the html file. You will always define all of your styles within this tag and you can have multiple styles defined within one style tag. To specify multiple classes on an element, just add a space between class names. If we were to create a new class called myClass2 that makes font italic and underlined, we could make our *Bolded Red Text* paragraph apply the style by updating its class attribute to be class="myClass myClass2".

Tip   Which CSS type to use? As a general rule of thumb, if there is any potential whatsoever to reuse a certain set of styling, make an external style file and add it there in a class; if there is no way to reuse the style outside of this page, use embedded CSS by adding it to the <style> tag; and if it only makes sense for this very specific line, use inline styling with the style attribute.

It is possible to get very granular with styling, as well as very broad. A developer can apply a style to a single element with only a specific ID, or it can be appled to all elements of a certain type. For example, let us make all <p> tags have underlined text, and make all <a> tags size 14 font. The updated embedded CSS and html file would look like Listing 4-5.

Listing 4-5. Updated helloHTML.html File with CSS Definitions Within Style Tag

```
<html>
        <style>
                .myClass {
                        font-weight: bold;
                        color: red;
                }
                .myClass2 {
                        font-style: italic;
                        text-decoration: underline;
                }
                p {

                        text-decoration: underline;

                }
                a {

                        font-size:14pt;

                }
        </style>
        <h1>Hello HTML!</h1>
        <h2>My name is Michael</h2>
        <h3>HTML is awesome!</h3>
        <p>This is a paragraph element</p>
        <b class="myClass">This is bold text</b>
        <i>This is italic text</i><u>This is underlined text</u><br/>
        This is text on a new line<br/><br/>
        Two             lines                   lower
        <br/><br/>
        <a href="http://google.com">Take me to Google!</a>
        <p class="myClass myClass2">
                Bolded Red Text
        </p>
</html>
```

Hello HTML!

My name is Michael

HTML is awesome!

This is a paragraph element

This is bold text *This is italic text*This is underlined text
This is text on a new line

Two lines lower

Take me to Google!

Bolded Red Text

Figure 4-4. *Updated helloHTML.html page with embedded styles*

You can see in Figure 4-4 that our link to Google is bigger and the *Bolded Red Text* paragraph element is now also italic and underlined by myClass 2, and the *This is a paragraph element* element is also underlined by the styling applied to all <p> elements. This brings us to the **Cascading** part of the name of CSS, which is not our primary focus, but suffice it to say that in CSS, elements will always keep the styles they inherently have unless they are overridden by a lower "cascaded" style. In this scenario, our *Bolded Red Text* is actually already underlined by the inherited style from the <p> style definition, but because myClass2 (which is a later style definition) does not conflict with it, it remains underlined. If myClass2 had a style definition of `text-decoration:none;`, then this particular <p> element would not be underlined, since that particular style would be overridden by the cascade despite <p> being defined as always underlined. Do not worry about understanding the cascade styling for the purposes of this text, but I encourage you to learn more about CSS for the *Salesforce Developer Pro* title.

Tip   As with HTML element attributes, there are many CSS styles that can be modified depending on the element you are working with. A quick online search will provide you with all the details you may need about which styles are available for a given element, and in some cases, what acceptable values are for that style.

HTML to Visualforce

Up to this point, this entire chapter has been devoted to getting you familiar with HTML and CSS. However, you are here to learn how to be a Salesforce developer! In the chapter introduction, it was mentioned that Visualforce is a markup language that is very similar to HTML. Although this is true, Visualforce actually takes it one step further. A Salesforce developer will write Visualforce code, which is proprietary and specific to the force.com platform, but when someone views the page, the force.com servers do some magic and actually present the user's browser with an HTML page rendered from that Visualforce. You may be asking, "What is the point then? Why not just write it in HTML?" This is a valid question, and the answer is: "Because Visualforce accelerates your development by allowing you to reuse Visualforce components which do a large amount of work for you and can interact with the data stored in Salesforce." That being said, you can still use HTML within Visualforce. Let us turn helloHTML.html into a helloVF Visualforce page.

Creating a Visualforce Page

All of the IDEs have a fairly similar approach to creating new Visualforce pages; this approach consists of setting up your force.com project and selecting "New" and "Visualforce Page". For this exercise, let us use the Developer Console. Begin by logging into your dev org.

1. Go to `http://login.salesforce.com` and log in

2. Open the Developer Console by clicking your name and selecting "Developer Console" (Figure 4-5)

3. Next, select "File", then "New", and "Visualforce Page" (Figure 4-6)

4. Name the page *helloVF* and click OK (Figure 4-7)

5. You should see what is in Figure 4-8, which is the generic boilerplate template for Visualforce pages.

Note   You may see a different API Version in the drop-down; this is OK.

Figure 4-5. *Launching the Developer Console*

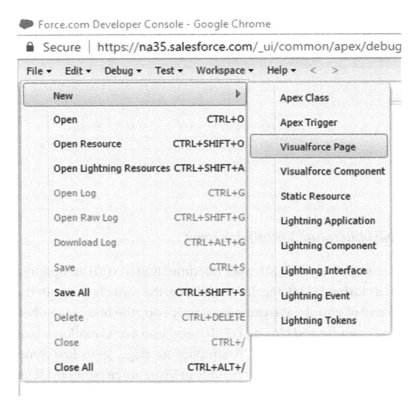

Figure 4-6. *Creating a new Visualforce Page*

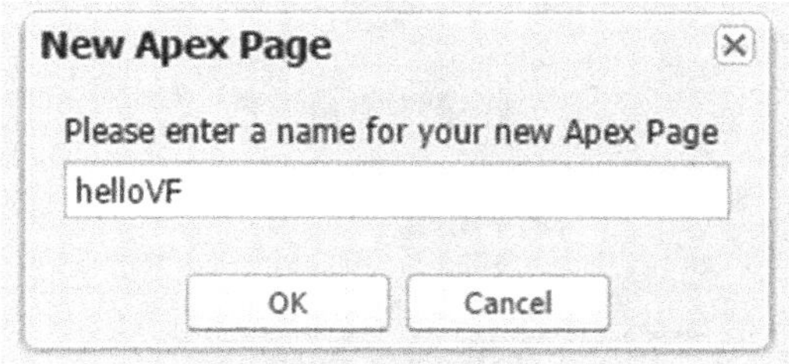

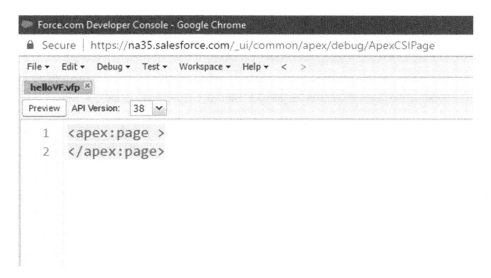

Figure 4-7. *Naming a new Visualforce Page*

Figure 4-8. *New boilerplate Visualforce Page*

From HTML, recall that all HTML page documents start with an opening HTML tag and end with a closing HTML tag. In Visualforce, the same is true, but the tag is <apex:page> instead of <html>. We can now simply copy the body of our helloHTML page (omitting the opening and closing HTML tags) into our Visualforce page and we should see the same resulting page. To simplify our page, let us first remove the default sidebar and header that Salesforce adds to Visualforce pages by default; these are the navigation items of Salesforce, the actual sidebar and header of Salesforce. We can remove them, as well as the default style sheets that Salesforce uses, by adding the attributes **showHeader**, **sidebar**, and **standardStyleSheets** to the page element like Listing 4-6.

Listing 4-6. helloVF Page Code

```
<apex:page showHeader="false" sidebar="false" standardStyleSheets="false">
        <style>
                .myClass {
                        font-weight: bold;
                        color: red;
                }
                .myClass2 {
                        font-style: italic;
                        text-decoration: underline;
                }
                p {
                        text-decoration: underline;
                }
                a {
                        font-size:14pt;
                }
        </style>
        <h1>Hello HTML!</h1>
        <h2>My name is Michael</h2>
        <h3>HTML is awesome!</h3>
        <p>This is a paragraph element</p>
        <b class="myClass">This is bold text</b>
        <i>This is italic text</i><u>This is underlined text</u><br/>
        This is text on a new line<br/><br/>
        Two             lines                   lower
        <br/><br/>
        <a href="http://google.com">Take me to Google!</a>
        <p class="myClass myClass2">
                Bolded Red Text
        </p>
</apex:page>
```

If you now click the *Preview* button in the Developer Console (Figure 4-8), you will be taken to the page as rendered by the force.com servers for your viewing pleasure (Figure 4-9).

Hello HTML!

My name is Michael

HTML is awesome!

This is a paragraph element

This is bold text *This is italic text*This is underlined text
This is text on a new line

Two lines lower

Take me to Google!

Bolded Red Text

Figure 4-9. *Rendered helloVF Visualforce page*

You are probably curious what happens if we add the sidebar, header, and standard style sheets back in, huh? Well, let us try it and see (Figure 4-10) by changing all the falses to true:
`<apex:page showHeader="`**`true`**`" sidebar="`**`true`**`" standardStylesheets="`**`true`**`">`.

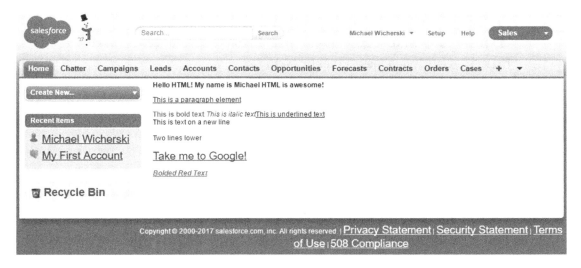

Figure 4-10. *helloVF page rendered with default sidebar, header, and style sheets*

Not quite what you were expecting, right? So what happened here? Why does everything look really bad and helloVF slightly different? This brings us back to the cascading styles. By setting styles directly on all <a> and <p> elements in our page, which is later in the cascade, we overrode those style properties of the other <a> and <p> elements on the page already provided by Salesforce. Our page, in turn, looks different because of standard Salesforce styling taking over our page in situations where we did not specify a style; our elements inherited styling. Again, this is not something to worry about much for the beginner's book, but if you are planning to pick up a copy of *Salesforce Developer Pro*, you should invest some time into understanding what happened and why—learn CSS a bit more in-depth.

The reason I keep stressing that a strong understanding of CSS is not necessary for this book is because the remainder will use mostly standard Visualforce styling and components with very minimal, if any, actual CSS. This is part of the beauty of Visualforce as opposed to writing **vanilla** (plain) HTML.

Visualforce Components

Akin to HTML element tags, Visualforce is structured through the use of **Visualforce Components**. A **Component** is a reusable element tag which may have a large amount of functionality built into it. Visualforce provides dozens of these components, as well as a mechanism for developers to create their own, which will be covered in the *Salesforce Developer Pro* title. Like HTML tags, components are capable of having attributes to help describe them, and sometimes these attributes are even required in order to use the component. Components also allow the developer to pass through attributes to the rendered HTML to control things normally controlled by HTML, for example: **styleClass** is the corresponding Visualforce Component attribute for the HTML **class** attribute. Let us create a proper Visualforce page, called *properVF* (Listing 4-7) without any vanilla HTML to see some components and how they style the page automatically in Figure 4-11.

Tip   Although Visualforce is case-insensitive, it is always best practice to try and write your code as case-sensitive. This will also help immensely when and if you start using CSS and JavaScript on your pages as CSS selectors (class names) and JavaScript code are case-sensitive.

Listing 4-7. properVF Visualforce Page Source Code

```
<apex:page>
    <apex:sectionHeader title="New Page" subtitle="Proper VF"/>
    <apex:pageBlock title="This is a Page Block" mode="maindetail">
        <apex:pageBlockSection title="This is a section with 2 columns">
                <apex:pageBlockSectionItem>
                        <apex:outputLabel>My Label</apex:outputLabel>
                        <apex:outputText>My Text</apex:outputText>
                </apex:pageBlockSectionItem>
                <apex:pageBlockSectionItem>
                        <apex:outputLabel>My Label</apex:outputLabel>
                        <apex:outputText>My Text</apex:outputText>
                </apex:pageBlockSectionItem>
        </apex:pageBlockSection>
        <apex:pageBlockSection title="This is a section with 1 column"
        collapsible="false">
                <apex:pageBlockSectionItem>
                        <apex:outputLabel>My Label</apex:outputLabel>
                        <apex:outputText>My Text</apex:outputText>
                </apex:pageBlockSectionItem>
        </apex:pageBlockSection>
    </apex:pageBlock>
</apex:page>
```

Figure 4-11.   *Rendered properVF page*

Look at all that included styling! The Visualforce Components, with some minimal attributes specified, have allowed us to create a styled and well-laid-out page in seconds. Let us go over the components used in this page to understand how we got to where we are:

- <apex:**page**> This is the required root element of all Visualforce pages. Since no attributes are specified here, all the defaults are in effect.

- <apex:**sectionHeader**> This component allows the quick creation of a page title with an icon to represent where the user is in the system. For example, if you were to look at an Account or Contact page, you would see a different icon for each: specifically, a folder for Accounts and a person's head for Contacts.

  - Title - this attribute is the smaller text on the upper part of this component.

  - Subtitle - this attribute is the larger, lower text of this component, contrary to its name.

- <apex:**pageBlock**> This is the primary content wrapper component. You will almost always want to start your page content wrapped within a pageBlock, as this gives you access to child elements of pageBlock such as pageBlockSection, pageBlockTable, pageBlockButtons, etc.

  - Title - this is the title text on the pageblock, very prominent.

  - Mode - this attribute has a specific set of values it will accept and controls the look of the pageBlock. maindetail is the common styling for "view" pages, while edit would be used for "edit" pages such as when creating or editing records.

- <apex:**pageBlockSection**> This is always a subcomponent of pageBlock, though it does not have to be a direct child (meaning it can go between the opening and closing tags of other components), as long as it is within a pageBlock. This component provides a collapsible section of the page, which can also handle column

wrapping for you on a left-right-left-right model when multiple columns are specified (meaning if you add two elements, it will put element 1 on the left, and element 2 on the right; adding four elements would make it go 1:left, 2:right, 3:left, 4:right.)

- Title - this is the title of the section. If a title is not specified, then the collapse option is not available.

- Columns - this specifies the number of columns in this section. Although there is no official restriction, it is recommended to stick to either one column or two for styling purposes and to ensure proper appearance across different screen sizes.

- Collapsible - if a title is specified, you can disable the ability to collapse the section. The collapsing feature is enabled by default (except when within an edit mode pageBlock, where this feature is unavailable).

- <apex:**pageBlockSectionItem**> This component must be a direct child of pageBlockSections and allows for the control of the two columns within every pageBlockSection item. The two columns of every item in a pageBlockSection are the label and the value.

- <apex:**outputLabel**> This is a text output component that styles your text as a label.

- <apex:**outputText**> This is a text output component that is the simplest text output format.

Note   Since all standard Visualforce components start with *apex:* the remainder of this text will omit that portion of the tag in the interest of readability. This means that when you see "create an outputText" component, it will be understood that the correct syntax to do so is `<apex:outputText>` and not `<outputText>`.

A few other components that are not in the preceding sample code, but are used very frequently, are the following:

- <apex:**form**> This creates a form element, which allows the developer to expose input components to capture user input. All input-type components must be within a form component.

- <apex:**pageBlockButtons**> This component must be a direct child of pageBlocks. It has an attribute for location which can be set to top, bottom, or both, allowing the developer to control where the buttons appear on a pageblock. We will see more of this later.

- <apex:**inputField**> The most valuable input component there is. Based on which field you assign to it, it will adapt the way it is displayed, the input it can accept, and the validation that happens on that data. It is extremely powerful and we will get very familiar with it shortly.

- <apex:**outputField**> The counterpart to inputField. OutputField is an extremely adaptable output component that will format your output data based on the type of data that it is; for example, a date or currency, rather than just printing plain text.

Tip   If input or output fields are confusing to you, try opening Excel or Google sheets or similar, and seeing how the cells differ when you type in a date or currency into a "General"-type cell vs. how they are presented and behave when you set the cell style to "Date" or "Currency" first.

Merge Fields

Up to this point, we have been exploring how to create **static** pages: pages where the content does not change. In today's world of digital media and considering how fast information moves and changes, it is very important that we build pages, and applications, which are **dynamic;** the more dynamic, the better. **Dynamic** pages change their content based on variable information which could include things such as screen size (think of how something looks on your desktop vs. your tablet or phone), time of day (think of the welcome message on some websites: "good morning" vs. "good evening"), or even just the data being pulled into view. With **dynamic** pages, a developer creates templated layouts and specifies conditions for which template to use and when. Let us start simple and create a new page that will welcome the currently logged-in user by name and also display the current date and time. Go ahead and make a new Visualforce page (Listing 4-8); I called mine *userWelcomePage* and it can be seen in Figure 4-12.

Listing 4-8. Visualforce Code for userWelcomePage

```
<apex:page>
    <apex:outputText value="Welcome {!$User.FirstName}"/><br/>
    <apex:outputText value="This page was loaded at {!NOW()}"/>
</apex:page>
```

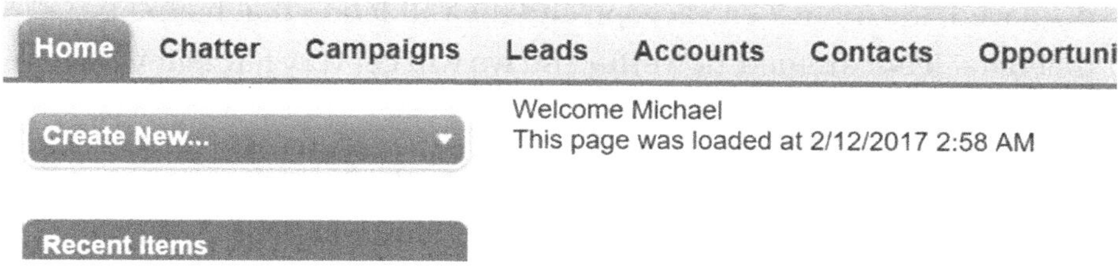

Figure 4-12. *userWelcomePage rendered*

Notice the **merge fields** included on this page for the user's name as well as the current time. The format for **merge fields** is {!mergeItem}. They always start with {! and end with }. Everything in between these characters is considered to be a merge **variable**—a reference to a specific value which can vary. Variables are very similar to the concept of "*x*" in math: it can equal 5 or 10, depending on the situation. When programming, variables can be used to represent anything, from data to database objects and more; this will be explained in more depth in the next chapter. Typically, in order to use a variable, you have to first set a value. However, there are a handful of **global variables**, meaning they are always available anywhere you are within Salesforce. User is one of these global variables. You can reference global variables by adding a $ in front of the variable name you are attempting to merge in. In Listing 4-8, this is done for {!$User.FirstName} to merge in the **context user** (user running the page) variable and display their first name. You could also reference their last name, email, phone, username, and so forth by changing FirstName to the field you want.

The second merged value on the page is the current time, {!NOW()}. This is actually a **function** which returns a variable. We'll cover functions (or **methods**) in the next chapter, but for now, just know that a function returns a value when used; in this case, the current time. You could also use a function like UPPER ('my lower case text') to return a converted text string which reads *'MY LOWER CASE TEXT'*. To merge that into a Visualforce page then, you would use {!UPPER('my lower case text')}. See Listing 4-9 for updated userWelcomePage code which includes a few more functions,

like CASE(), which allows you to return specific values in specific cases. In this case, we are converting the number of the month, 1 being January, and 12 being December, that is returned by the **MONTH** function into the text name of the month.

Listing 4-9. Updated userWelcomePage Code

```
<apex:page>
    <apex:outputText value="Welcome {!$User.FirstName}"/><br/>
    <apex:outputText value="This page was loaded at {!NOW()}"/><br/>
    <apex:outputText value="This means it is day {!DAY(TODAY())} of
                            {!CASE(MONTH(TODAY()),1,'January',2,
                            'February',3,'March',4,'April',5,'May',6,
                            'June',7,'July',8,'August',9,'September',10,
                            'October',11,'November','December')}
                            of the year {!YEAR(TODAY())}"/><br/>
    <apex:outputText value="{!UPPER('my lower case text')}"/>
</apex:page>
```

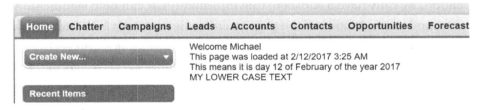

Figure 4-13. *Updated userWelcomePage rendered*

Tip   Remember that HTML, and Visualforce, consider multiple whitespaces as a single whitespace, allowing developers to structure their code for readibility without affecting the output on the page.

Standard Controller

Although you are now able to create your own Visualforce pages and know how to merge in data, unless you are planning to just create pages using globally accessible information, you are going to need some way of interacting with the database.

This brings us back to the MVC framework, as it is time to move on from View to **Controller**. Visualforce controllers come in two official versions as "controllers": standard and custom. There are also custom **extensions**, which always extend the controller. That is to say, they are not stand-alone controllers, but instead extend the standard controller with additional functionality, and a controller can be extended by multiple extensions. So what is a **Standard Controller** then?

A **Standard Controller** is provided by the force.com platform for every database object automatically. It allows the creation of a simple custom Visualforce page to control the view or editing of records of that type of object or viewing records related to a specific record of that type of object. For example, an Account Standard Controller would allow the developer to pull in all fields on an Account for editing or viewing, but also display that Account's Contacts or Activity History for view only. The Standard Controller also provides basic functions such as Save, Cancel, Edit, and View for the specific record it is being used with.

A good sample use case for a custom Visualforce page using a Standard Controller would be to present a simplified page when a new record is being created. Oftentimes, objects start getting bloated with massive amounts of fields to collect data, but at the time of creation, we only have a subset of that information. It can help significantly speed up data entry, and user adoption, if the page to create new records is slimmed down to only the relvant information, cutting down on searching for fields and verifying that everything has been filled out. For example, looking at Figure 4-14, we see all the data that could be collected about an Account record. This is likely all important information, but assume that you will only ever know the company name, phone number, and maybe the website. It would be much easier to create new accounts if that was all that is presented to you on the new record page. We will use the Standard Controller to make a page just like that and also include the description field in Listing 4-10.

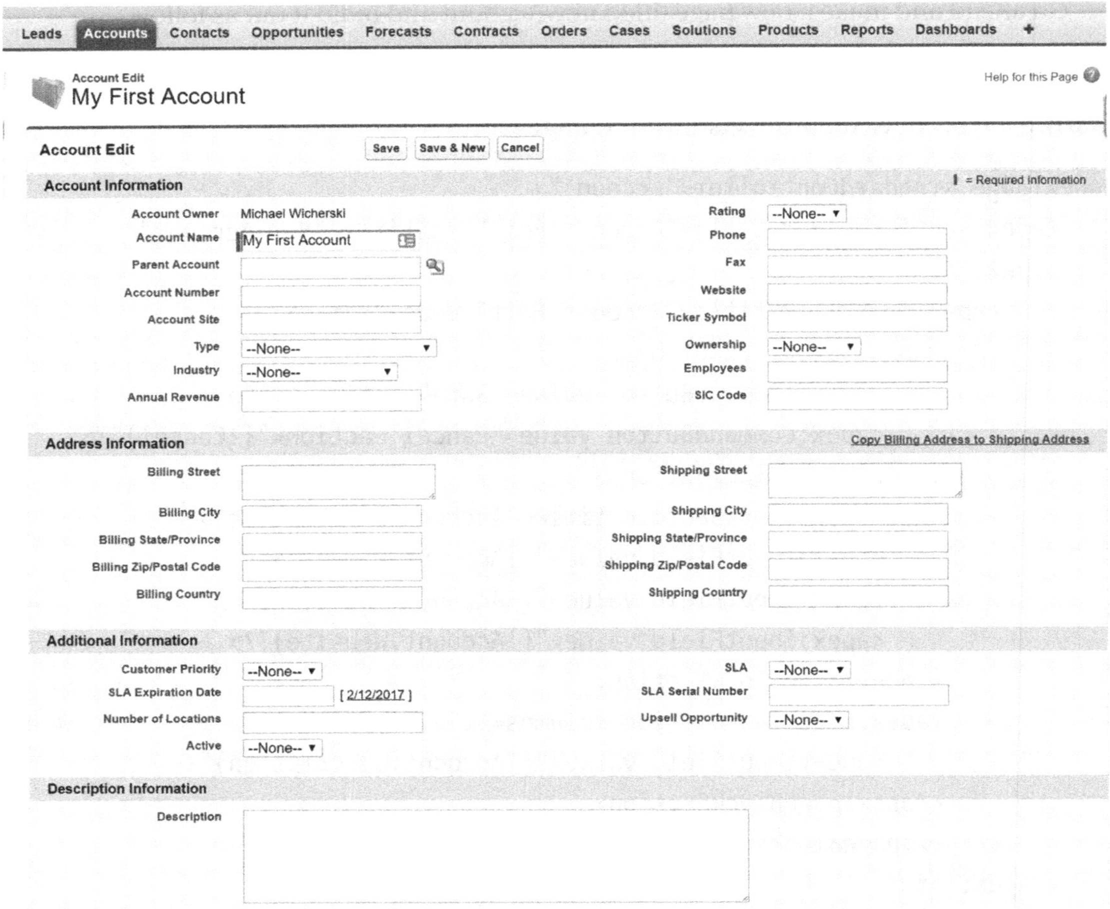

Figure 4-14. *Account edit page*

Note   If your goal is to override the standard buttons such as New and Edit or View for an object, you must use a Standard Controller. Likewise, if you plan to embed your page into an object's page layout, you must also use a Standard Controller for that object.

Go ahead and make a new page titled newAccount and build it out as follows (Figure 4-15).

Listing 4-10. newAccount Visualforce Page Code

```
<apex:page standardController="Account">
    <apex:sectionHeader title="Account Edit" subtitle="New Account"/>
    <apex:form>
        <apex:pageBlock title="Account Edit" mode="edit">
            <apex:pageBlockButtons>
                <apex:commandButton value="Save" action="{!Save}"/>
                <apex:commandButton value="Cancel" action="{!Cancel}"/>
            </apex:pageBlockButtons>
            <apex:pageBlockSection title="Account Information">
                <apex:inputField value="{!Account.Name}"/>
                <apex:inputField value="{!Account.Phone}"/>
                <apex:inputField value="{!Account.Website}"/>
            </apex:pageBlockSection>
            <apex:pageBlockSection columns="1">
                <apex:inputField value="{!Account.Description}"/>
            </apex:pageBlockSection>
        </apex:pageBlock>
    </apex:form>
</apex:page>
```

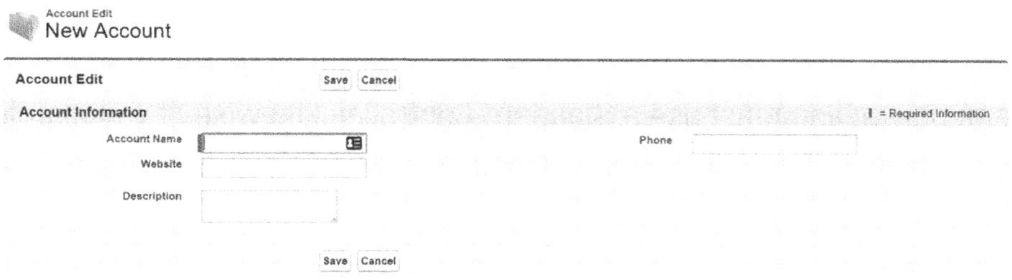

Figure 4-15. *Custom newAccount page rendered*

Hopefully, this is all coming together, and you were able to follow along with why and how this page was built out. Our sectionHeader component, and entire page, adopted the Account styling scheme because we specified the Account Standard Controller. The Standard Controller also provided us with the Account variable for use in our merge fields. The pageBlock component has been set to the edit mode, further styling the page as an edit page, including the pageBlockSections. The inputField components adapted to the field type that was being passed in: the name field is required by the database, so it is automatically required here; description is a long text area field type, so it displays as a larger area than regular text fields. Let us clean this page up a bit for easier data input and introduce a tab order, that is, the order in which the Tab key takes you (it defaults to left-right, just like fields are laid out, but we want to go top-down then over). We will also add the lookup field for parent account in case we wish to set it during creation and change the description field to use inputTextArea and change its size. All of this is shown in Listing 4-11 and Figure 4-16.

Listing 4-11. Updated newAccount Visualforce Page Code

```
<apex:page standardController="Account">
    <apex:sectionHeader title="Account Edit" subtitle="New Account"/>
    <apex:form>
        <apex:pageBlock title="Account Edit" mode="edit">
            <apex:pageBlockButtons>
                <apex:commandButton value="Save" action="{!Save}"/>
                <apex:commandButton value="Cancel" action="{!Cancel}"/>
            </apex:pageBlockButtons>
            <apex:pageBlockSection title="Account Information">
                <apex:inputField value="{!Account.Name}" tabOrderHint="1"/>
                <apex:inputField value="{!Account.ParentId}" tabOrder
                Hint="4"/>
                <apex:inputField value="{!Account.Phone}" tabOrder
                Hint="2"/>
                <apex:pageBlockSectionItem/>
                <apex:inputField value="{!Account.Website}" tabOrder
                Hint="3"/>
            </apex:pageBlockSection>
            <apex:pageBlockSection title="Description Information"
            columns="1">
```

```
                <apex:inputTextArea value="{!Account.Description}"
                cols="80" rows="5"
                tabIndex="50"/>
            </apex:pageBlockSection>
        </apex:pageBlock>
    </apex:form>
</apex:page>
```

Tip   When mixing inputField and the other input elements such as inputText or inputTextArea, if you wish to set the tab order, you must multiply the index number by 10 for the non-inputField fields. This is a system quirk that has been responsible for many a hair-pulling tantrum.

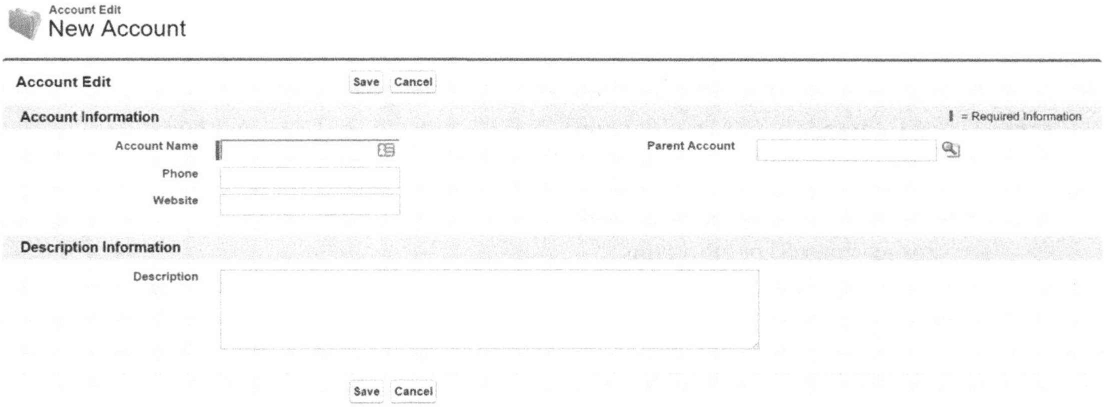

Figure 4-16.   *Updated newAccount Visualforce page rendered*

We now have our simplified Account creation page, but we still need to set it as the page that gets invoked (used) instead of the default new page. To do that:

1. Click *Setup*

2. Navigate to *Accounts* under the *Customize* section of *Build,* or use the Setup Search

3. Select *Buttons, Links, and Actions*

4. Click the "*Edit*" link on the row corresponding to the "*New*" button

5. Set the "*Override With*" value to "*Visualforce Page*" and select "*newAccount*" from the drop-down. See Figure 4-17.

6. Click *Save*

Tip   Notice that although there are many other Visualforce pages you have created, only the newAccount page shows up as an option to override the New button on Accounts. This is because the newAccount page is the only one to use the Account Standard Controller.

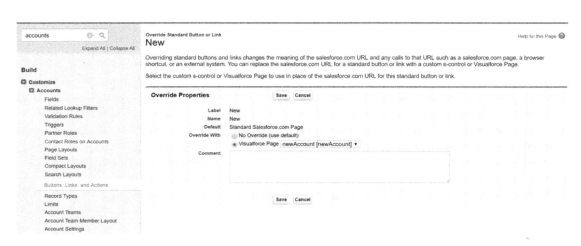

Figure 4-17. *Setting newAccount as the page override for the default New button for Accounts*

If you were to now go to the Accounts tab and click New, or any other location where a "New" button or link is available for an Account object, you will be taken to your custom page.

Summary

For some of you, this chapter was a complete breeze, for others, it was the most difficult thing you have attempted in a long time. To both, congratulations on sticking through it. With the basics of HTML and Visualforce added to your developer toolkit, you are now well prepared to start developing custom pages for Salesforce.com apps allowing for custom viewing as well as editing of data.

There will undoubtedly be quirks that you will run in to that will take some time to resolve, especially once you start using CSS, but there is a great sense of satisfaction that comes from finally figuring it all out. In Chapter 5, we will take a look at the Apex programming language to close the MVC circle with the ability to customize each part. I would recommend taking this moment to take a breather, grab some coffee (or tea if that is more your cup of... tea), and play with basic Visualforce for a while to really get the basics locked in. Perhaps work through the examples in this chapter on a different object like Lead?

CHAPTER 5

Introduction to Apex

If Chapter 3 needed a cup of coffee or tea, this chapter is going to need a pot, or two. The importance of this chapter cannot be stressed enough, as it will lay the groundwork for all future chapters across this book, and the rest of the series. This chapter is going to introduce the Apex programming language: Salesforce's own proprietary language.

We will see how to create Apex classes and how to write methods, and we will learn about all of the little components that make up the language such as variables, flow control, structure, and even governor limits. Fair warning: this chapter is going to be mostly walls of text, as short as possible, but no pop-up pictures here, folks. Without further ado…

Apex

The lifeblood of Salesforce developers around the globe, Apex, is a very interesting language. It's an object-oriented language, strongly typed, but developers typically take a more procedural approach when developing with it. Read on to make your head stop spinning (hopefully).

"Strongly typed" means that the language is very particular about many things, and has its quirks. It is a very high-maintenance relationship between developer and machine, but in exchange, there is far less ambiguity, and more robust feedback from the IDE than with loosely (weakly) typed languages. Strongly typed languages will enforce the "types" of values being used (we will cover this in the Variables section of this chapter), as well as ensuring that your methods (also called functions, and covered later in this chapter in the Methods section of Classes) are being used with the correct parameters.

© Michael Wicherski 2017
M. Wicherski, *Beginning Salesforce Developer*, https://doi.org/10.1007/978-1-4842-3300-9_5

Object-oriented and procedural progamming styles determine the way in which a developer's code is laid out. In pure object-oriented programming (OOP), the objects carry with them data as well as their related functionality within the object. This contrasts with the procedural style wherein procedures (also called functions or methods) are created which act on data that is given (passed) to it and execute a sequence of procedures or actions (also called statements). We have already seen that objects as they are defined with regards to the database and objects in Apex are very similar, except in addition to the data they carry, they can also have functionality applied to them. We will see this in the Classes section of this chapter.

Apex is very similar in syntax (the arrangement of keywords, phrases, and characters to create well-formed code) to Java. If you have any previous experience with Java, JavaScript, C, C++, or any other OOP language, then Apex should be very easy for you to pick up. There are some minor syntactical differences, but overall the structure is similar enough. Apex does have one perk (some consider it a curse) which the other languages lack, and that is that it is case-insensitive; this means that "tHis PHrAse" is the same as "ThIs pHraSe".

Statements

When programming, everything you write is essentially an instruction to the computer. Instructions can also be called commands, but are usually referred to as statements. Statements make a definitive statement to the computer describing either what you want it to do, or what your expected result is after it performs the action. Different languages have differing syntax, but in many languages, the syntax for a statement is to terminate (end) each statement with a semicolon (;). Statements typically span only a single line, but can be broken into multiple lines depending on how the language handles whitespace.

In Apex, you can break queries onto multiple lines as well as call methods and pass their parameters on separate lines without any special accomodations. Collections of statements can be made within functions (or methods), and these will be covered in the next sections. Listing 5-1 provides examples of statements which declare and/or assign values to variables (covered in the next section).

Listing 5-1. Sample Statements

```
String firstName = 'Mike';
Date todaysDate;
Integer five = 5;
```

Comments

When writing code, sometimes you will run into sections which are obscure by nature. This could be a very complex evaluation, or maybe it is a mathematical formula that you want to leave the reference and variable explanation in your code so you can easily refer to it when making edits months from now. You could also have a section of code that you want to temporarily disable for one reason or another. Comments come in handy for these situations. They allow you to write notes in your code which do not affect the execution of your code, or wrap a section of code into a comment block to prevent its execution. Anything marked as a comment will simply be ignored while the application is executing. There are two ways to write comments: single-line and multiline. Although you can use the single-line way to comment out multiple lines, this is frowned upon and typically results in more time spent commenting/uncommenting. Single-line comments are marked by using two forward slashes //. Multiline comments are marked by using a forward slash and asterisk /* to open the comment block, and closing the block is done with an asterisk followed by a forward slash */. Multiline comments should seem similar to opening and closing tags in HTML and Visualforce. Examples of comments follow in Listing 5-2.

Listing 5-2. Comment Examples

```
/*This is an example of a multiline comment block.
Notice that only the first
and last lines have the markings.
For readability, it is also acceptable to have the opening and closing
marks on separate lines, but you can have them like the opening mark. This
closing mark is on a separate line.
*/

/*
```

```
    Multiline comments can also be used to comment out sections of code, by
turning them into a comment
    <commented code here>
*/

String firstName = 'Mike'; // single-line comments can be made after
                              //statements on the same line
String lastName = 'Wicherski';
//they can also be made on separate lines
//typically to explain what happens next
//this is a second single-line comment
//the following variable stores full name
String fullName = firstName + ' ' + lastName;

// multiline comments can also comment out sections of a statement
String interestingUseCase = /* 'some value no longer desired' */ 'new
desired value';
```

Variables

If you have ever taken algebra, you will surely have strong emotions about the phrase "Solve for *x*." Whether these emotions are positive or nauseating sentiments, you have already used variables before, perhaps without knowing it. *x* is, in fact, a variable; as you may have guessed, a variable simply represents a value which can vary, and is typically—or at least preferably—accompanied by a friendly identifier (word or words). Variables allow their user (in this case developers) to store data that can then be acted upon. In mathematics, variables are the letters of the alphabet, or special characters such as π (pi). In modern programming languages, words can be used to make it easy to understand what value is stored in a given variable. For example, if you were writing a form, you might store the value of the person's first name in a variable called firstName. Likewise, you could store their last name in lastName, email in email, date of birth in birthday, and so on. Storing a value in a variable is done by assigning the value, and assignment is done using the equals sign (=). For example, using the assignment statment, firstName = 'Mike';.

Tip   Naming your variables in such a manner that is easy to understand is beneficial to everyone. It allows you to develop quickly without pausing to remember what is stored in a given variable, and it also allows other developers to understand your code faster. Using a variable name of asdf to store the value of someone's first name from a form would be rather cryptic.

In the examples provided, the names and email are text values, but the birthdate is a date. With strongly typed languages, such as Apex, this must be distinguished when creating your variable by specifying the type. You can specify the type when declaring (creating and/or setting the value of) your variable by typing something like `String firstName;` and `Date birthday;`. On the other hand, in loosely typed languages such as JavaScript, this would be a nonissue and you would simply declare your variables like this: `var firstName;` and `var birthday;`. We will see more about types in the following sections.

Tip   If you have used a spreadsheet program such as Microsoft Excel or Google Sheets, it may be helpful to think of variable types as the data type for your columns. If you set a column type to text, it will just be text. If you set it to Date, then based on your formatting of the cell, typing 1/1/1900 might appear as Jan-1, Jan 1990, or any other Date format. Likewise, if you set a column to one of the numeric types, such as currency or number, the formatting changes from that of plain text and adds separator commas and the decimal point.

Primitive Data Types

Primitive data types are basic pieces of a programming language that include built-in support. In most languages, these types cannot be modified and are used as basic building blocks to construct application logic. The primitive data types in Apex are as follows:

- Blob - a collection of binary data. Typically used to represent the data of files. Can be converted to String (see String) and vice versa as needed.

- Boolean - variables of this type can only be assigned as true, false, or null (see Null).

- Date - represents a date and contains no time data.

- Datetime - represents a specific point in time. For example, timestamps. Contains information about both date and time.

Tip   Datetime values are stored in the force.com database in UTC time. However, when querying this data and displaying on a Visualforce page using the outputField component, the value is calculated based on the current user's timezone setting on their profile.

- Decimal - A number with a decimal point. The default type for Currency fields. Decimal variables have an arbitrary precision (number of digits after the decimal point) which is set when the decimal value is first assigned, unless explicitly set.

- Double - A very large number which can include a decimal, with a minimum value of -2^{63} and maximum value of 2^{63}-1. Should only be used for very large numbers and complex calculations. See also Long.

- ID - Any valid 18-character Force.com record ID.

Tip   If you set a variable of type ID to a 15-character value, Apex will convert it to the corresponding 18-character ID automatically. Be careful though, this will not work if you set a variable of type string to a 15-character ID, Apex will leave that alone.

- Integer - A whole number, meaning there is no decimal point, which can range in value from -2,147,483,648 through 2,147,483,647.

- Long - Similar to double, but does not contain a decimal point; it's the same as an integer, but can be used to represent much larger numbers than an integer. Use this if you need to represent a number outside the range of integers only. Long values can range from -2^{63} through 2^{63}-1 (that is a really big number!).

- Object - This is a special variable type which can be used to represent any other type, including user-defined objects (we will see this later). However, before actually performing any action on an Object variable, it must be converted (cast) to a specific type.

- String - Any set of characters, such as a word, surrounded by quotes. String is arguably the most versatile type (other than Object) as it can be cast to most other types, and is easy to store and manipulate. Strings have no limit on a maximum length, but the Heap Size Limit is used to control the program's size. The Heap Size Governor Limit will be covered in the Governor Limits section of this chapter.

Note   An empty string (no characters) is not the same as a null string. It is perfectly acceptable to assign the value of '' (empty string, not even a space) to a string variable—this is simply an empty value.

- Time - represents a particular time. Can only be used with system methods (very limited use cases).

- Null - Although null is technically not a primitive type per se, it is a special constant value that is used to represent "nothing". All variables declared, but not assigned a value, have the value of null assigned automatically.

Caution   A very common mistake by new developers, and even veterans, is to assume that a boolean variable is assigned the value of false if no value is set. In Apex, all variables, including booleans are initialized as null until a value is assigned.

Constants

Constants are really just simple variables. What makes them special is that their values are set in stone once they are set. In other words, once you set a value for a constant, you cannot modify it. This is useful in certain applications, for example to set the number of rows displayed in a table to the user. If you always want there to be five rows, you can set this at the start of your program and never have the need to change it. Constants are defined using the final keyword as in Listing 5-3.

Listing 5-3. Examples of Constants

```
final integer numberOfRows = 5;

/*remember they can only be set once, but do not have to be set when
declared*/
//the following is also acceptable
final integer altNumberOfRows;
altNumberOfRows = 5;
```

Arithmetic, Concatenation, and Unary Operators

In addition to the simple assignment operator (=), programming languages have to provide for the ability to perform arithmetic operations and to modify data stored in variables. These actions are made possible, in part, through the arithmetic, concatenation, and unary operators.

Basic Arithmetic and Concatenation

- \+ The additive operator. Used to perform addition with numerical values. Also used to concatenate (merge) text strings together. For example, to merge my first name, a space, and my last name together: `'Mike' + ' ' + 'Wicherski'`

- \- The subtraction operator. Used to perform subtraction with numerical values.

- * The multiplication operator. Used to multiply numerical values.

- / The division operator. Used to divide numerical values.

- % The remainder operator. Also called modulo. Performs division, but the returned value is the remainder of the operation only. Therefore `5%2 = 1.`

Compound Assignments

Compound assignments can be formed by combining the basic arithmetic operators with the assignment operator =. Compound assignments are shorthand for performing arithmetic with a variable if you are doing a simple operation. For example if you are

adding 5 to x (assume $x = 1$ already), you could do $x += 5$ and after this, x would be 6. This is equivalent to writing $x = x + 5$.

- $+=$ Compound addition assignment $x += 5$, same as $x = x + 5$

- $-=$ Compound subtraction assignment $x -= 5$, same as $x = x - 5$

- $/=$ Compound division assignment $x /= 5$, same as $x = x / 5$

- $*=$ Compound multiplication assignment $x *= 5$, same as $x = x * 5$

Unary Operations

Unary operations are ones where only one operand is used, basically a single input. For example, taking the number 2 and making it negative. You do so with the unary minus operator - (commonly known as a minus sign). So -2 is the unary operation of making 2 a negative number. In programming, you also have a unary operator to turn booleans into their opposites, called the not operator !. !true is false and !false is true.

- - Unary negation operator. Used to negate a value.

- ++ Increment operator. Used to increment a variable's value in a single statement. For example, $x++$; increments the value of x by one.

- -- Decrement operator. Used to decrement a variable's value in a single statement. For example, $x--$; decrements the value of x by one.

- ! Not operator. Also known as the logical complement. Inverts the value of a boolean. For example, !true is equivalent to false, and !false is equivalent to true.

Note   Although the unary positive operator + also exists, and could be used to set a value as +1 (positive one), numerical values are assumed to be positive and the unary operator is therefore not necessary.

Composite Data Types

Composite data types, also known as compound data types, are data types which may be included natively in a programming language along with built-in support, or are types which can be defined and constructed by the developer. Composite data types are typically assembled from primitive data types and/or other composite

types, and creating our own composite type will be covered in the Classes section of this chapter. Collections, or aggregate data types, are also considered to be composite data types.

Collections

Collections are composite data types which allow the developer to aggregate, or collect, multiple other types into a single variable. The collection types available in Apex are List, Set, and Map.

List

A list (also called an array) is a variable representing an ordered collection of elements which are distinguised by their indices. The index of a list is numeric, and starts at 0 - always. This means that if you have one item in your list, then that item's index is 0. If you have two items, the first item's index is 0, and the second item's index is 1. This will become clearer and less confusing the more you use it. A list can be a collection of any data type, primitive or otherwise. A list is declared by specfying the type of element it collects. For example, `List<String> myListOfStrings` could be used to represent a collection of strings. Therefore, in order to declare a list variable, you would type *list*, followed by the type collected within < >. In order to retrieve the value of an element at index 0, you can do `String retrieved = myListOfStrings[0];`

You can also quickly instantiate (declare and define) a list to be a collection of results from a query (see Chapter 3). For example, if you wanted to have a list of your Account records, you could do something like `List<Account> myAccountList = [select ID, name from Account];` to create a list containing an unfiltered list of your accounts with the ID and name fields available.

Set

Sets are similar to lists in that they are collections of elements. However, they are unordered (you cannot access their values by index), and are special because they cannot contain duplicates. If you attempt to add the same value to a set twice, there will still only be one element in the set with that value. This makes sets ideal for maintaining a collection of unique elements, such as IDs or emails, when operating with large data sets. A set is declared the same way a list is, except the set keyword is used instead of list, like so: `set<String> mySetOfStrings`.

Note   A set is a collection of unordered elements, and you cannot use an index to retrieve an element like you can with a list. Also, when iterating through the elements in a set, you should not rely on the order being the same.

Map

Maps are what are known as "key/value" pairs. They are collections which index their values using a specific key. So where lists are ordered in the order they are built, with the first element being at index 0, the second at index 1, and so on, maps are indexed by a key you specify. Both the keys and values in a map can be any data type, meaning they can be primitive, composites, collections, and user defined. For example, if you had a map that had a String type as both the key and value, you could add an element to the collection with key "firstName" and a value of "Mike". Then, when you wanted to retrieve the value of "firstName", you would use "firstName" as the index. Maps are declared by using the keyword map followed by the type of key and the type of value, like map<key,value>. To declare our map containing the first name value, we would then use `map<String,String> myStringMap`.

As with lists, you can use a quick statement to instantiate a map to the results of a SOQL query, which would map a record to its corresponding ID. For example, with the same Account query as used in the list example, map<ID, Account> myAccountMap = new map<ID, Account>([select ID, name from Account]); would create a map of your Account records indexed by their corresponding IDs. Note that the results of a query are always a list, and it is really the map data type's constructor that is building our map from the list. We will cover constructors in the Classes and Methods sections later in this chapter.

Tip   You can quickly instantiate a list or map from the results of a query in a single-line statement. For lists, this can be a direct assignment, and for maps, you pass the query result list into the map's constructor method.

Enum

An Enum is a special type of collection variable, really a special data type in its own right (and it is also a type of inherent constant). Where the other types can have elements added to or removed from them, an Enum is set in stone once it is created. They are used

to define variables as options which never change. For example, there are four seasons, and only four seasons. If we were writing an application that had a use for specifying a season, we could create an Enum called "Seasons", with the available values as Winter, Spring, Summer, and Fall. The declaration and definition (or assignment) of an Enum are different from all other variables, in that you never have to use an equals sign (=) to assign the value. You simply declare Enums with their values defined like this: Enum Season {`Winter, Spring, Summer, Fall`};. If you want to access the value, you now use the dot notation (using a period or dot) like this—Season.Spring or Season. Fall—instead of how you would access an element in a list or map by using its index.

Flow Control

Flow control is a very important aspect of programming. It is what allows the developer to specify the order in which the application should flow, or in other words, what order things happen in. In any given application, it is rare for events to always happen in the same order; there are typically any number of conditions that could cause one thing to happen instead of another, or maybe there is an extra step to take, or a step that should be skipped. Flow control can be exacted on the application logic in a number of ways.

Flow control can be performed using sequential, selection, or repetition controls. Another way of affecting flow control is through methods (or functions), covered in later sections. All flow control, with the exception of sequential control and methods, is performed using logical operators to form evaulation statements.

Logical Operators

Logical operators allow the developer to check whether or not certain criteria evaluate to true or false, and to then make decisions about the application's flow based on the result. They are similar to mathematical arithmetic operators. There will be some sample expressions at the end of this section in Listing 5-4.

- == (equals) checks if the left value is equivalent to the right value
  - 5==5 evaluates to true
  - 5==6 evaluates to false
- != (not equal) checks if the left value is not equivalent to the right value
  - 5!=5 evaluates to false

- 5!=6 evaluates to true
- < (less than) checks if the left value is less than the right value
    - 5<6 evaluates to true
    - 6<5 evaluates to false
- <= (less than or equal to) checks if the left side is less than or equal to the right side
    - 5<=5 evaluates to true
    - 5<=6 evaluates to true
    - 6<=5 evaluates to false
- > (greater than) checks if the left side is greater than the right side
    - 6>5 evaluates to true
    - 5>6 evaluates to false
- >= (greater than or equal to) checks if the left side is greater than or equal to right side
    - 6>=6 evaluates to true
    - 6>=5 evaluates to true
    - 5>=6 evaluates to false
- && (and) checks if both the left and right side are true
    - true && true evaluates to true
    - true && false evaluates to false
    - false && true evaluates to false
    - false && false evaluates to false
- || (or) checks to see if at least one of the left or right side is true
    - true || true evaluates to true
    - true || false evaluates to true
    - false || true evaluates to true
    - false || false evaluates to false

- ! (not) special operator that negates the given value (flips it).

    - !true evaluates to false

    - !false evaluates to true

Listing 5-4. Some Sample Expressions

```
(a > 0 && b > 0 && c > 0) // true when a,b, and c are positive values

(a < 0 || 0 > b || c < 0) /*true when at least one of a,b, or c is a
negative value*/

/* true when 2+2=4 AND 5==5 AND either 6 is greater than or equal to 5 OR 4
is greater than 5. (this is true as written)*/
((2+2 = 4) && 5==5 && (6>=5 || 4>5))
```

Short Circuit Evalation

When using the AND and OR operators (&& and ||) there is a feature called short circuit evaluation. Short circuit evaluation allows developers to optimize their logic as well as prevent some errors during execution. For example, if an evaluation statement is a || b and a is true, then there is no need for the application to evaluate b, since we already know the expression will evaluate to true. Similarly, for the expression a && b, if a is false, there is no way for the expression to ever be true, so we can short circuit and move on. This becomes extremely useful if your expression contains division for example. If your expression is a/b == 5, but b=0, then you would get a fatal error (causing your program to break) because division by 0 is not allowed. You could prevent this problem using short circuit evaluation by first testing to ensure that b is not equal to 0: (b != 0 && a/b==5).

Sequential

The most straightforward way to affect flow is sequential control, and this simply means that the application executes its programmed logic one line at a time, top to bottom. This can be seen in the code snippet (short piece of code, possibly taken out of context) in Listing 5-5, which will set three String variables to construct my full name.

Listing 5-5. Sequential Control Example

```
String firstName = 'Mike';
String lastName = 'Wicherski;
String fullName = firstName + ' ' + lastName;
```

Selection

Selection controls determine which sequence, or branch, of code should be executed. Selection controls are also known as "if/else" branches, as they mimic the thought process that goes into them. "If A is true, then do X, else (otherwise), do Y)."

If/else

If/else statements are fairly self-explanatory. If this, then that, otherwise (else) that. They are a way for developers to essentially implement flow charts into the application logic. They can be expanded with as many branches as necessary by adding in an else if statement. So the structure is really if, else if, else. The final else is actually not necessary. It is a way to specify an action if none of the other branch criteria are met, but if it is omitted, the application simply continues sequentially. If statements have the syntax of the keyword if (or else if, or else) followed by the criteria within parentheses and all of the statements which should be executed if the criteria evaluates to true within curly braces. Listing 5-6 provides an example.

Listing 5-6. Example if/else

```
if(x < 0){
    // x is negative
}
else if (x > 0) {
    // x is positive
}
else { /*IMPORTANT NOTE: The final else statement does not have any
criteria, ever*/
    // x is zero
}
```

Tip   If you have a very short if statement, or your if statement only executes one command, you can omit the curly braces and simply write `if (condition) thenStatement;` However, for readability it is best practice to always include the curly braces. If you do use this syntax, it is best practice to at least put the statement to execute on its own line.

Flow controls can also be nested, one within another, and we frequently see this with selection controls. If one set of general criteria is met, you may have a whole other set of logic subbranches to evaluate to determine the absolute best path to take as demonstrated in Listing 5-7.

Listing 5-7. Example Nested if/else

```
if(x < 0){
    // x is negative
    if (x < -100){
        // x is a large negative number
    }
    else {
        // x is a small negative number
    }
}
else if (x > 0) {
    // x is positive
    if (x > 100){
        // x is over a hundred!
    }
    else if ( x > 1000)
        /* x is over a thousand! (not using curly braces for this single
        statement!)*/
    else
        /* x is less than 100 (also not using curly braces for this single
        statement)*/
}
// don't want to do anything when x = 0, don't need the final else
```

Switch

Switch-case statements are essentially cleaner ways of representing larger if/else if/
else branches. Unfortunately, Apex does not support them, but there are rumors/posts
from legitimate sources that make it sound like this feature is coming soon, so we will
cover it here, using the Java syntax since Apex is very similar syntactically. Switch-case
statements are simply shorthand, allowing you to specify the evaluation statement
just once, and then specifying each result and the action when that result is true. For
example, compare the if/else branch with the corresponding switch-case that follows in
Listing 5-8.

Listing 5-8. If/else Compared to Switch-Case

```
//if statements
if (season == 'Winter'){
    // do something Winter specific
}
else if(season == 'Spring'){
    //do something Spring specific
}
else if (season == 'Summer'){
    // do something Summer specific
}
else if (season == 'Fall'){
    // do something Fall specific
}
else {
    // the variable season does not contain a valid value
}

//switch-case
switch (season){
    case 'Winter':
        //do something Winter specific
        break; /*the keyword 'break' is covered in the section for
        Repetition control*/
    case 'Spring':
```

```
        //do something Spring specific
        break;
    case 'Summer':
        //do something summer specific
        break;
    case 'Fall':
        //do something Fall specific
        break;
    default:
        //the variable season does not contain a valid value
        break;
}
```

Ternary

Ternary statements (operators) allow the developer to write a single if/else branch statement on a single line. This is considered shorthand, and while it may make development easier and allows for writing less code, it also lowers the readability aspect. This should be taken into consideration in larger applications and its use should be limited. This also becomes a concern when writing test coverage (Chapter 9), as in order to write proper test coverage, every branch should be tested, and ternary operators make it more difficult to verify this (since they are on a single line). A ternary statement has the following syntax: (if criteria)?(if_true):(if_false). However, only the first parentheses are needed. For example, to assign the value of a boolean, we could use the following statement: boolean isFive = (5==5)?true:false;. The boolean isFive would only be set to true if 5 is really equal to 5, and false otherwise. This could be written as the if/else statement in Listing 5-9 as well.

Listing 5-9. Longhand Version of Ternary Example

```
Boolean isFive;
if (5==5){
    isFive = true;
}
else {
    isFive = false;
}
```

> **Tip**   A chained ternary statement can be used to cleanly mimic switch-case functionality when calling functions when the criteria evalautes to true. This can also be done using if/else branches.

Repetition

Repetition controls are blocks of statements in which the same statements are repeated as long as a certain criterion, or set of criteria, are satisfied. Repetition controls are typically used when the same actions (statements) should be performed on multiple elements—typically stored in a collection. The three forms of repetition control are for loops, while loops (also known as while-do loops), and do-while loops. For loops can also be thought of as iterative (rather than repetitive), as they advance themselves by their nature, causing them to be inherently iterative—repetitive, but moving along to the next element with each repetition. In contracts, within the two versions of while loops, there has to be an explicit statement which will progress the application logic forward to the next element, or to terminate the loop, in order to avoid becoming stuck in an infinite loop. Read on to learn when to use each type of loop.

> **Caution**   Infinite loops are very dangerous, as they have the potential to completely bog down a system. Luckily, on the Force.com platform, there are governor limits which will automatically stop your loops after a certain time. However, this also means that your code will not work, so you must still make every effort to avoid infinite loops.

for

For loops are most useful when the number of iterations is known, or can be deduced; for example, if you know you want to run a set of statements ten times, or if you have a list of elements, and want to run the statements against all members of the list. There are three ways to define a for loop flow control: a set number of iterations, index notation iterating over a collection, and element notation iterating over a collection. The syntax for a for loop is typically the keyword for, followed by a variable to hold data for evaluation in the criteria, which is then followed by criteria which must evaluate to

true for the loop to continue to the next iteration, and a "step" argument which modifies the evaluation criteria. All statements executed in each iteration of the for loop are then enclosed within curly braces. Examples of each type of for loop are provided in Listings 5-10, 5-11, and 5-12.

Listing 5-10. For Loop with a Set Number of Iterations

```
//In the following example, i is our control variable
/*Start with i equal to 0, and continue while i < 10, increment i by one
every iteration*/
for (Integer i = 0; i < 10; i++){
    //do something
} // perform  i++ after completing the loop and evaluate for criteria again
```

Listing 5-11. For Loop over a Collection of Elements Using Index Notation

```
// Here i is our control variable again
// myList.size() provides the number of elements in myList
for (Integer i=0; i< myList.size(); i++){
    /*to access the elements in the list for each iteration, the index
    notation can be used*/

    myList[i] = someValue;

    /* notice that i would contain an integer capable of representing an
    index in this case*/
}
```

Listing 5-12. For Loop over a Collection of Elements Using Element Notation

```
/* shorthand notation to iterate over every element within myList
NOTE: element here is meant to be any data type capable of being in a
collection*/
for (element e : myList){
    // in this notation, e is already selected as the element from the array
    /* there is no need to use index notation to reference the element of
    the current iteration*/
}
```

while (do)

While loops are best used for situations when you do not know the number of repetitions necessary. For example, when parsing (reading) a document, you do not know how many lines there are in it. Using a while loop, you can use logic such as "if there is a next line, keep going". A common example of this is the XML (eXtensible Markup Language) Stream Reader, which is used to parse XML documents. Remember that while loops need to be manually advanced, and so, in this example of reading XML documents while there is a next element, you must tell the application logic to advance to the next element somewhere within the loop. Typically, this looks like Listing 5-13.

Listing 5-13. Sample While Loop for the XML Stream Reader

```
//assume all necessary instantiation and assignment is done
XMLStreamReader reader;

    /* We will cover methods in later sections of this chapter, but for
    the purposes of this example, just know that reader.hasNext() is
    either true or false, depending on whether or not the reader has a
    next element*/

while (reader.hasNext()){ /* while the criteria in parenthesis is true,
enter the loop*/

    reader.next(); //this method advances the reader to the next element

    /* At this point we have tested that the reader has a next element
    in the while loop criteria, which entered the loop. We have now also
    advanced to that next element using next()*/

    //do something now that we have advanced

    /* We have reached the end of the loop. Now that the loop is done,
    re-evaluate again whether or not reader.hasNext() and repeat the loop
    again if it does*/
}
```

do-while

A do-while loop is exactly the same as a while (or while-do) with the exception that it always executes the repetitive statements at least once. Essentially, it executes once first, then checks the criteria of the loop to see whether or not it should loop again, and then loops as necessary. Using our previous example of an XML reader, this would look like Listing 5-14.

Listing 5-14. Sample Do-While Loop for the XML Stream Reader

```
//assume all necessary instantiation and assignment is done
XMLStreamReader reader;

do { //do the following once

    reader.next(); //this method advances the reader to the next element

}
while (reader.hasNext()); // if the criteria evalautes to true, loop again
```

Caution   Be very careful with assumptions when using do-while loops. In the given example, we are making the assumption that the reader has at least one element. If the document is empty, this would not be true, and the application would break.

Break and Continue

Break and continue are two special keywords which are statements on their own. They allow the developer to control repetitive controls while within the loop, allowing them to either break out early, or skip over the remaining statements in the current iteration and progress to the next.

Break allows the developer to break out of the loop. This is useful if the developer wants to exit a for loop before all the elements have been iterated over, or if a special condition has been met and the loop should stop executing right here, right now. This can be used when searching for a specific element in a collection and breaking out upon finding it; for example, if you are looking for a specific Account by name in a collection of Accounts as in Listing 5-15.

Listing 5-15. Searching for an Account to Demonstrate Using Break

```
//assume this list actually contains some accounts
List<Account> listOfAccounts;
Boolean accountFound = false;
for (Account a : listOfAccounts){
    if (a.name == 'name searched for'){
        //flip our boolean to true since we found the account!
        accountFound = true;
        break;//break out of the loop to avoid unnecessary statements
    }
}
```

Continue allows the developer to cleanly express intended functionality. It can be used to instruct the execution flow to skip over the remainder of the current loop statements and continue onto the next element in a for loop or the next loop cycle within while loops. It comes in handy when using if/else branches within loops and providing for a special case where the loop should be continued, as opposed to breaking out, or continuing sequentially. Listing 5-16 shows a rather impractical, but valid, use case where the value of *x* will never be printed to the log.

Listing 5-16. Impractical While Loop with Continue

```
Integer x = 0;
while (true){ //continue running until otherwise specified
    x = x + 1;
    //single line if statement to continue to the next loop
    if (x < 100) continue;
    else if (x <100) system.debug(x); // print out value of x if x<100
    else if (x == 100) break; //break out if we hit x=100
}
```

Note   You have now seen curly braces several times in this chapter. Curly braces are always used when you want to group statements together. They can be used when grouping statements in flow controls such as if/else branches or loops, as well as when defining classes and methods.

Classes

Classes in programming, at a high-level definition, allow for the grouping of variables (also known as attributes when used in this fashion), methods, other subclasses, and any other functionality, or templating of the application or logic a developer may need to build their application. Classes are the actual files which store all Apex code on the force. com platform and you would have a file named fileName.cls, where cls denotes the class extension. In Apex, classes can also be triggers (covered in the next chapter), where the name and extension of the file are triggerName.trigger.

When writing classes such as the one in Listing 5-17, the class name is the first thing in the file and everything else is wrapped within curly braces. It is also common, and allowable, to include a lead-in multiline comment block to desribe the purpose of the class before this line. Comments used in this fashion are also known as documentation. Although Apex does not natively support generating documentation from specifically formatted comments, there are a number of third-party tools that can help with this if you are used to it and wish to continue doing so.

Listing 5-17. Very Basic Sample Class with a Nested Inner Class

```
/**
 * myFirstClass
 * This would be a description explaining what my class does
 * Notice the formatting of this comment block. It is common practice to
   use the /** to denote
 * the start of a descriptive comment rather than commenting out code
   temporarily / other uses
 * of comments. Every subsequent line is also started with similar
   indentation and a *
 */
class myFirstClass{
    //class attributes, classes, methods, etc. go here

    /**
     * myInnerClass
     * Can also describe inner classes using the documentation format
     */
```

```
class myInnerclass{
    // inner class attributes, classes, methods, etc. go here
}
}
```

Calling (using/causing to execute or run) class methods and variables (attributes) is done the same way you would access an Enum value, by using the dot notation. On the force.com platform, database objects behave like classes as well, which makes it easy to utilize both database objects as well as developer-defined classes in the same way—this lends itself to very readable code. Therefore, accessing an sObject field is done using dot notation as well; for example: Account.Name would access an Account sObject's Name field. If an Account were to be represented as a class, it would be done like Listing 5-18.

Listing 5-18. Mock Representation of an Account sObject as a Class

```
class Account{
    String Name;
    // other fields

    /* there are also functional (class) methods available for all
sObjects, see next sections*/
}
```

Methods

Methods, also known as functions, procedures, or subroutines, are collections of statements for the purpose of breaking down application logic into reusable chunks. This has a few benefits, not the least of which is improving the readibility of your code. Methods can be written in such a way that they can also take arguments (or parameters), which are variables or values passed in (provided to), upon which the method can act. There are different types of methods: functional (or class), constructors, and those which return a value.

Return Methods

Return methods are ones which are defined to return values of a specified type after having run. These methods can accept arguments, but do not have to. Return methods can return any data type. To define a return method, you would first specify the type of return, then the method name, and a comma-separated list of typed (specified type) arguments.

A good example of a method would be a method to check whether or not an email is valid as in Listing 5-19. You would pass the string representation of the email into the method, and the method would then evaluate it to true or false, and ideally return that value so that the application can act on it. If you are building an application that checks a number of email addresses, then you can see the benefit of having a reusable method that you can use to check the addresses rather than rewriting the statements each time.

Listing 5-19. Sample Using a Return Method to Check All Emails in a Collection

```
//assume the array is populated
List<String> emailAddresses;
for (String emailString : emailAddresses){
    // check email
    //call the checkEmail method and pass in the emailString
    checkEmail(emailString);
}

Boolean checkEmail(String input){
    if (input is a valid email){
        return true; //use the return keyword to return a value and exit
        the method
        // for return methods, you can short circuit and exit early by
        returning a value
        // this is similar to how break statements work, except a value is
        returned.
    }
    return false;
    /*the return false statement could be wrapped into an else branch,
    but it is not necessary*/
}
```

Constructors

Constructors are a special type of method. They are designed to "construct" a class. This means that they create a new instance of a class, and instantiate all variables and assign values as applicable, as seen in Listing 5-20. They can also be defined to accept arguments which can further be used to set attributes within the class upon

instantiation, like in Listing 5-21. The return type of a constructor method is the same as the name of the class.

Listing 5-20. Sample Class with Its Constructor

```
/**
 * sampleClass
 * A class to demonstrate a constructor setting the value for three
 variables.
 */
class sampleClass{
    Integer myNumber;
    String firstName;
    String lastName;

    sampleClass (){
       myNumber = 5;
       firstName = 'Mike';
       lastName = 'Wicherski';
    }
}

/*create a new instance of the sample class, and store it in the
myClassExample variable*/
sampleClass myClassExample = new sampleClass();
```

Listing 5-21. Sample Class with Its Constructor Taking in Arguments (Parameters)

```
/**
 * sampleClassParams
 * A class to demonstrate a constructor setting the value for three
 variables.
 */
class sampleClassParams{
    Integer myNumber;
    String firstName;
    String lastName;
```

```
    sampleClassParams (String fName, String lName){
       myNumber = 5; /* this is still hardcoded, not set from values
       passed in*/
       firstName = fName; /* sets this instance's firstName to the passed
       fName value*/
       lastName = lName; /* sets this instance's lastName to the passed
      lName value*/
    }
}

/* 1. create a new instance of the sample class, and store it in the
myClassExample variable*/
/* 2. pass in values to store in the variables of firstName and lastName
based on how the*/
// constructor is defined
sampleClassParams myClassParamsExample = new sampleClassParams
('Mike','Wicherski');
```

Function Methods

Function methods, also known as void methods or class methods, are ones which do not return any value and can either accept arguments or have no arguments. These methods are defined as part of the class and designed to be shared among all instances of the same class—see Listing 5-22. They are typically used to modify the instances of the class directly in some fashion, specifically the attributes.

Listing 5-22. Example of a Class Method to Set a Class Variable of an Instance

```
class myClass{
    String firstName;

    myClass(){} // instantiate the class, but set no values. Can be on one line

    // the void keyword can be used to define methods that return no value
    void setFirstName(string input){
       firstName = input;
    }
}
```

```
//instantiate the class
 myClass exampleVariable = new myClass();

// exampleVariable.firstName is currently null
exampleVariable.setFirstName('Mike');

/*exampleVariable.firstName is now 'Mike' because the method has executed
for this instance of the myClass class*/
```

The This Keyword

The this keyword is a pretty nifty little tool. It seems rather innocent, but it is very powerful in terms of manipulating scope (described in more detail a few sections down). It is a keyword that can be used to refer to the current instance of the class you are using it in, which allows functional (class) methods to reuse the same variable names already declared as class attributes to maintain readiblity, while being very clear and specific about which variable you are modifying. Listing 5-23 shows how to use the this keyword.

Listing 5-23. Example of a Class Method to Set a Class Variable of an Instance Using the This Keyword

```
class myClass{
    String firstName;

    myClass(){}

    void setFirstName(String firstName){
       /*The this keyword here, allows us to reference the firstName
       variable on THIS instance of the class. Which in turn, allows us to
       use the same variable name for the parameter of the function*/

       this.firstName = firstName;
    }
}
```

Coding Conventions

When writing code, there are a number of conventions that developers try to stick to in order to more or less have a set of standards. These are purely guidelines, but not following them tends to cause your peers to judge your code as messy and difficult to read.

camelCase

When naming variables, methods, classes, or anything really, if the name is longer than a single word, using camelCase is the preferred way to make your name readable. CamelCase simply means that every subsequent word in your name is capitalized. An example would be thisIsMyExampleVariable. Even though it is comrpised of multiple words, it is easy to read thanks to the capitalization of the first letter of each word, despite the lack of spaces.

Note   It is generally accepted as best practice to always name classes using UpperCamelCase, that is, camelCase where the first letter is also capitalized.

Names

It is always best practice, even for your own sanity, to use names for things that make sense to you. Using ddfh as a variable name probably does not have much meaning to you, and even if it is an acronym for some variable that currently makes sense, a few months down the line, you will not remember what this was. Using names such as firstName, birthDate, currentRecord, and so on promote readability and maintainability of your code.

Names should also never start with a number. 10digitId is cosidered to be a bad name, and in some languages, it is actually not allowed to start a name with a number. If you must absolutely start the variable name with a number, common practice is to preface the number with a single capital X character, giving you the name X10DigitId. Names should never start with a special character such as #, $, or %.

Classes, Methods, and Variables

Different languages have different conventions regarding the differences in naming of classes, methods, and variables; however, they almost always name classes in UpperCamelCase (first letter is capitalized and then camelCase). In Java, classes should be named UpperCamelCase and always be nouns, while methods and variables should be lowerCamelCase with methods being verbs. In my experience, developers tend to take a hybrid approach in Apex (the language lends itself to this).

In Apex, the trend I have seen is to follow the noun vs. verb conventions of Java, but I have not seen consistent use of the lower vs. upper camelCase conventions. Personally, I use a different methodology altogether when it comes to naming classes. If my class is going to deal with platform native functionality, such as facilitating a trigger, or acting as a controller or extension for a page, I name the class in lowerCamelCase. If the class is involved in external activities, or activities of a very specific kind, such as a batch, I prefix the type of activity in all caps, followed by an underscore and the activity; for example, BATCH_GeocodeAccounts or API_GoogleCalendar. My reasoning for this is that the force.com UI, and metadata API, sort the class names alphabetically by uppercase first, then by lowercase. This allows me to group my functionality together so I can easily find what I am looking for within large applications, the same as for method names. Of course, as these are all guidelines; feel free to develop whatever convention works best for you. The most important things is to be consistent! Without consistency, your organization will be messy and very difficult to follow, especially since you are not using a common convention.

Tip   It is considered courteous to make sure that you do not have extremely long statements on a single line. Years ago, it was convention to limit statements to 60 characters per line. However, today's developers have more screen space and 60 characters is extremely limiting when dealing with multiple nesting of statements. Keep it within reason and you should be fine. Most IDEs also have the ability to line wrap if needed, but this does not always result in the most legible code, so if you are working in a team, consider finding out or establishing what works for the team.

Constants

Constants are a special case when it comes to naming. Due to their immutable (unchangeable) nature, constants are typically named in ALL CAPS. This makes it very apparent that the variable you are using is a constant since no other variables are named in this fashion. Keeping in mind that Apex is case insensitive, using the variable does not really make a difference if it is not all caps, but it is still best practice to do so. Some developers like to prefix their constants with const_ to form const_variableName, which is also acceptable, but less widespread.

Indentation

The biggest pet peeve in reading code is if it is not properly indented. If you ever take a programming course in school, this can cost you dearly if done improperly. It is very easy to do, and is very important to get into the habit of doing it early on. The general rule of thumb is that a single tab should be used every time a new level of nesting is introduced. This allows the closing curly brace to vertically align with the opening statement line, allowing the reader to see at a glance how statements are grouped. Consider the following examples in Listings 5-24 and 5-25 with and without indentation.

Listing 5-24. Indentation Sample

```
//classes start left most
class indentationSampleClass{
    for (element e : elementArray){ /* every statement within the class
                                    should be indented once*/
        // every element within this loop should be indented an additional tab
        if (true){
            /*all elements in this if should be indented another
            additional tab*/
        }
    }/*this closing curly brace aligns vertically with the for statement,
        indicating the span*/
}/* this curly brase aligns vertically with the class opening statement,
    indicating span*/
```

Listing 5-25. Lack of Indentation Sample

```
class indentationSampleClass{
for (element e : elementArray){
//statement within the for
if (true){ // this if is within the for loop
//statement within the if
}
} /*can you tell which of these is the closing if, and which is the closing
    for, or class brace?*/
}
```

Scope

Scope is a concept that allows certain portions of application logic and variables to be hidden from other portions, or conversely, exposed outside of the application itself. The scope modifiers are private, public, and global—in order from most restrictive access to least restrictive. Normally, all attributes and methods of a class are private, and the class itself is also private. Attributes and methods of a class which are marked as private are only available within that specific class. Classes and attributes marked as public allow access to members across the same namespace, whereas global scope allows access from even outside of the namespace. Namespace is a concept that will be covered in the Salesforce Developer Pro title, but for now, just know that Apex assumes everything is private by default and most of the classes you will create will be elevated to public access.

Note   You cannot mark something as less restrictive than its container (what it is a part of). This means that you cannot have a global method inside of a public class or a public attribute inside of a private class.

Threads

A thread can also be referred to as a transaction or execution context. Transactions are very useful, but what are they? A transaction thread is quite simply the aggregate timeline of all execution activities that are cascade triggered by an action from invocation (start)

to completion. Take the following use case: a record is inserted into the database, this triggers a before insert trigger, the data is inserted into the database, this triggers an after insert trigger, which calls a method in a class to modify a different record, triggering another database update, and so on. All of these actions occur within the same chain, or transaction thread. Why is this useful? The force.com platform has a built-in feature for rolling back all database changes if the thread fails at any point, for any reason. This means that if you saved data to the database, then errored out further in the thread, those changes get rolled back (undone), and it is as if you never attempted to make the change.

Caution   Although the force.com platform offers native rollback functionality for threads, be very careful when communicating with external servers. If you perform actions on external servers, and your thread fails after that point, the rollback does not affect the actions completed on those external servers.

Governor Limits

As Apex executes on the force.com platform, which is run on a shared tenancy architecture, Salesforce imposes certain limits as to the level of resources consumed within a single thread by applications built on the platform. These limits are collectively known as Governor Limits. These limits affect a number of different things, but the most common ones are denoted here; what they affect or limit, and how to work around those limits, will be explained in greater detail throughout the remainder of the series.

Note   Remember, Governor Limits are subject to change, and tend to do so between releases. Any specific numbers provided in this chapter should be assumed to be general guidelines and subject to change.

Script Statements

This limit is also related to total execution time. It can really only be hit if you are performing a large number of loop operations. Typically, you would have to use nested loops several times or levels deep to hit this limit or to have an endless loop (but that is another problem entirely, and one you should fix quickly).

Heapsize

RAM, memory, heap: heapsize just means how much memory your application is taking up. This is a very rare error to run into unless you are actively manipulating files directly in your Apex code. Typically, operations like that are best offloaded to external services, but on occasion, it is something that can be done natively (on the platform). The current heapsize limit is 5MB, meaning that if you are manipulating files, your total memory use of the application (per thread) must be under 6MB, so your file has to also be smaller so as to leave room for logic.

Queries

Queries against the database have two separate limits to watch out for. First off, you may only perform 100 query actions against the database in total per thread. This is a total per thread: it does not matter how you break your code up across classes or methods, it will all count together as long as it occurs within the same thread. This is also true for the other query limit regarding the number of rows which can be retrieved from the database. The cap on rows retrieved in total in a single thread is 50,000 rows (records).

DML

As with query limits, there are two different DML (Data Manipulation Language) limits. DML statements are any statements which directly interact with the database to write to it. This includes inserts, updates, deletes, and undeletes. In a single thread, there can be a total of 150 DML statements, affecting a total of 10,000 rows.

Callouts

A callout is a request to an external server over the Internet. At present, a single thread can execute 100 callouts, with a total processing time of two minutes across all callouts combined.

Future

Future methods are very special kinds of methods used to invoke asynchronous processing and will be covered in detail in the *Salesforce Developer Pro* title of the series.

A Large Sample

There have been many concepts introduced throughout this chapter. Listing 5-26 exemplifies many of them for reference.

Listing 5-26. A Large Sample Class Containing Many of the Concepts Covered in This Chapter

```
/**
 * chapter 5 class containing chapter 5 concepts
 */
public class Chapter5{
        String firstName;
        Integer five = 5;
        String lastName;

        public Chapter5(){ /*constructor, assume it is invoked for this
        demo*/
                if (true){
                        firstName = 'Michael';      //set firstName
                }
                for (integer i= five; i<=10; i++){ //increment five to 10
                        five++;
                }
                firstName = getShortName(); /*set firstName to returned
                value of method*/
                setLastName('aLastName');    // call class method
                String fullName = firstName + ' ' + lastName; /*concatenate
                                                    string*/

                do{ //do while
                        five--;
                }
                while (five > 5);

                while (five < 10) {         //while do
                        five+=1;
                }
```

```
        boolean bool = true;
        while(true){
                if (!bool == false){ //not operand
                        bool = false;
                        continue;
                }
                if(true) break; //if you get this far, break
        }
    }

    public void setLastName(string lastName){ // class method
        this.lastName = lastName;
    }

    private string getShortName(){ //return method
        return 'Mike';
    }
}
```

Summary

If you have made it this far, congratulations. This chapter is essentially a comp sci 101 course crammed into under 30 pages. It is the cornerstone of the rest of the series and everything that we will do from now on, so if there are any parts you are not sure about, go reread that section—or even do some Google searches for some more samples. If you are more of the hands-on type, and learn by doing, then Chapter 6 has plenty of that in store for you. See you there.

CHAPTER 6

Apex Classes and Triggers

Time to put all that theory from Chapter 5 to good use. This chapter will focus on the creation of class (and trigger) files and understanding when they are needed.

Classes

Classes are the basic building blocks of your application logic. They are containers to be used for storing your Apex code which can be used to build custom object definitions, create methods (functions), define attributes, and so much more. Triggers are also a type of class, but are special and handled differently on the force.com platform, so they get their own section. For now, we will focus on creating generic classes, such as a utility class which can be reused by other classes.

Creating a Class

The first step to writing Apex code in a class is to create the class itself, naturally. For this example, we will be using the Developer Console (Figure 6-1) once more, and then move on to the desktop IDEs after that when creating our classes.

1. Log in

2. Open the Developer Console by clicking your name ➤ Developer Console

3. File ➤ New ➤ Apex Class

4. Name this class "util"

© Michael Wicherski 2017
M. Wicherski, *Beginning Salesforce Developer*, https://doi.org/10.1007/978-1-4842-3300-9_6

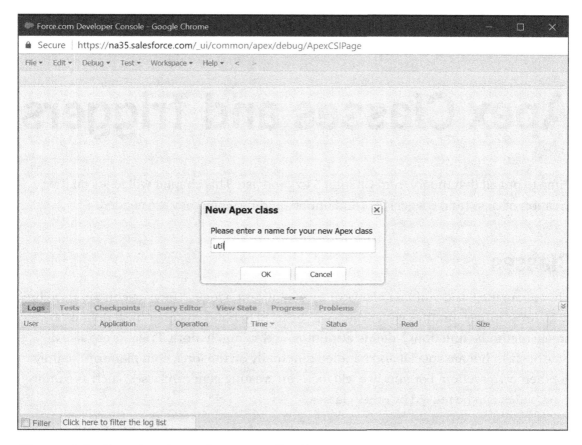

Figure 6-1. *Creating Apex class named util*

You will notice that the creation of this class also prepopulates some code for you (Figure 6-2). All classes are defined this way, and have modifiers added on this first line. In this case, we have a scope modifier added already, defining the class as a public class; this will be true for the majority of classes you will create. Recall from Chapter 5 that the other options for this are Private and Global, but these are covered in more depth in the *Salesforce Developer Pro* title. There is another very common modifier that is included for classes in Apex: sharing. "With sharing" and "without sharing" are modifiers that are added to classes which control what data the code contained in those classes can access. All this means is that if your organization has Contacts defined as private sharing model for example, then someone using this class would only be able to affect Contacts which they have access to if "with sharing" is used to define the class. If the class is defined as "without sharing", however, the user would be able to affect Contacts that they do not normally have access to as the sharing model would be ignored. This setting also applies

to object-level and field-level security settings in addition to the sharing model. The `with sharing` modifier must be explicitly set, since Apex by default runs in the system context (`without sharing`).

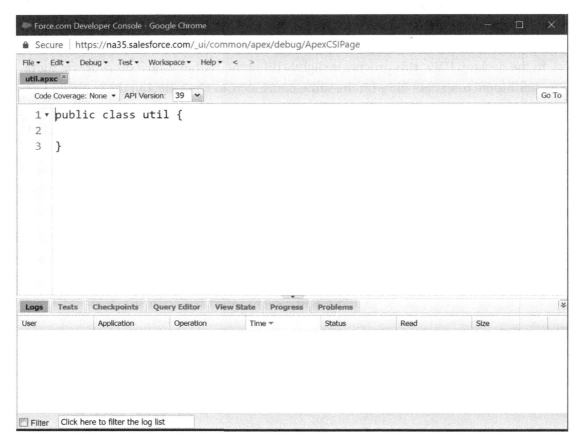

Figure 6-2. *New util Apex class*

A few other things worth noting in Figure 6-2 are the code coverage and API version settings of this class file. We will cover Test Coverage in Chapter 8, but know that you can quickly reference it here when opening the class file from the Developer Console. As for API version, this is how a developer can ensure backward compatibility across new releases of Salesforce. Every release of Salesforce (Fall, Winter, Spring) brings with it a new API version. When you create a new class (or page), the then-current API version is automatically selected, granting you access to all of the newest features. However, if there are features which you need to use for some reason, such as other,

older, classes (or pages), you can modify the API version here to a previous version. This will, unfortunately, prevent you from using any new features that were released in an API version higher than the one you select. It is also possible to raise the API version of existing classes, - provided that class is not utilizing any features which were deprecated in the version you are transitioning to. Salesforce does not autoupdate your existing classes/pages to a higher API version with each release.

In the desktop IDEs, this process is slightly different. Rather than a drop-down, there is an additional metadata file with the same name as your class file, but the extension ends with -meta.xml. Metadata is simply "data about data," in this case data about the class, which itself is data stored on the force.com servers. Figures 6-3 and 6-4 show what this metadata file looks like in the Eclipse IDE. Changing the API version would be a simple matter of changing the number between the <apiVersion> opening and closing XML tags to the desired API version and then saving that file back to the server.

> ⌄ 🗁 src
> > ⌄ 🗁 classes
> > > 🅧 util.cls
> > > 🅧 util.cls-meta.xml

Figure 6-3. *Class meta definition file for util.cls in as seen in Eclipse IDE*

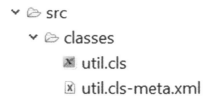

```
util.cls-meta.xml ⊠
1 <?xml version="1.0" encoding="UTF-8"?>
2 <ApexClass xmlns="http://soap.sforce.com/2006/04/metadata">
3     <apiVersion>39.0</apiVersion>
4     <status>Active</status>
5 </ApexClass>
6 |
```

Figure 6-4. *Contents of the util.cls-meta.xml file as seen in Eclipse IDE*

Note   The API version can be changed for your purposes, but it is important to note that newer features will be unavailable. You can also update the API version of your existing files as they are released as long as there are no deprecated features being used.

Tip   A great way to keep up to date with all the new features released and/or deprecated with each release is to review the release notes. Salesforce provides these well in advance of upcoming releases, and also notifies you of the opportunity to upgrade your sandbox(es) to the new release prior to its official release into the production environments. Keeping this in mind will allow you to proactively test and upgrade your code, and possibly even optimize it by using new features.

Methods

In Chapter 5, we briefly touched on constructor methods and how they allow a developer to construct and instantiate a class, but they are not always necessary. For this particular example of a utility class, we do not need to construct the class—we want our utility functions (methods) to be always available and independent of the other functions within the class. To achieve this functionality, we will be using another special keyword: static. Static variables and methods do not require an instance of a class in order to run or be used, exist independently of all other nonstatic (instance) variables and methods, cannot access instance variables or methods, and exist only within the scope of the transaction (thread). Recall from Chapter 5 that a transaction, or execution thread, is the series of actions which occur as a result of an action. A static variable or method existing only within the context of its transaction is significant because this means that if two records are inserted in separate actions, for example, each one would have its own static version of the variable or method, which prevents unwanted sharing of data and errors.

Chapter 5 also showed us how to create methods, define their return types, and define their parameters. One of the methods we will be adding to our utility class (Listing 6-1) will allow us to reverse the order of a list of sObjects. Recall from Chapter 3 that sObjects are the generic objects which can represent any Salesforce object, standard or custom. The reason we are going to use the generic sObject, rather than a specific type of Salesforce object such as an Account, is that this allows our method to be more dynamic.

Listing 6-1. reverseSOBjectList Method to Reverse the Order of sObject in a List

```
/**
 * A utility method to reverse the order of sObjects within a list collection
 * @param  input list<sObject> which contains the list of sObjects to reverse
 * @return list<sObject> which is a generic sObject typed collection of the
   reversed list
 */
public static list<sObject> reverseSObjectList(list<sObject> input){
  list<sObject> temp = new list<sObject>();
  for (integer i = input.size()-1; i>=0; i--){
    temp.add(input[i]);
  }
  return temp;
}
```

You can see in Listing 6-1 for reverseSObjectList that the method is defined as public, static, with a return type of list<sObject>, and accepting a parameter of list<sObject> which gets assigned to the local method variable of input. Next, we instantiate a temporary list of sObjects that we will be using to work with. We can then iterate (in reverse order) over the input list and add each element in turn to the temp list. Once we are finished, the temp list is returned as a list of sObjects. Notice that we start the iterator integer i as equal to the size of the input array minus one. Why the minus one? Recall that lists are indexed starting at 0. This means that the size of the list is always larger by one than its highest index. If you try to set i=input.size() and execute the preceding code, you will get an exception that the index is out of bounds. The for loop then decrements the iterator variable until it is equal to 0, which is the lowest possible index in a list. While many programming languages have a method built in for lists (or arrays) called reverse to perform this functionality, Apex does not—but now we have our own!

Utility Class

Enough with the teasing already! Let us assemble our utility class now. We can start by taking the preceding reverseSObjectList method and placing it in our class. Your code for the util class should now look like Listing 6-2.

Listing 6-2. Util Class with reverseSObjectList Method Contained Within It

```
/**
 * util.cls
 * A collection of utility methods
 */
public class util{

  /**
   * A utility method to reverse the order of sObjects within a list
     collection
   * @param  input list<sObject> which contains the list of sObjects to
     reverse
   * @return list<sObject> which is a generic sObject typed collection of
     the reversed
   *  list
   */
  public static list<sObject> reverseSObjectList(list<sObject> input){
    list<sObject> temp = new list<sObject>();
    for (integer i = input.size()-1; i>=0; i--){
      temp.add(input[i]);
    }
    return temp;
  }
}
```

Tip   Remember to keep your code indented and commented properly!

Another commonly used method is one which converts a number into a string with a certain number of digits; for example, changing 9 into 09 or 009. This is extremely useful when naming records and sorting them afterward. If this is not done, then lexicographically, the strings of numbers would be sorted as 0, 1, 10, 11... 2, 20, 21... 3, 30, 31..., and so on. By prepending the 0 to numbers lower than 10, we ensure that the sorting order will be 0, 01, 02, 03... 10, 11, 12... 20, 21... 30, 31..., and so on. See Listing 6-3 to see how to do this in Apex.

Listing 6-3. Code for the twoDigitIntegerString Method

```
/**
 * twoDigitIntegerString
 * @description Returns a 2 digit string representation of integers by
   prepending 0 if under 10
 * @param integer input
 * @return string representation of input
 */
public static string twoDigitIntegerString(integer input){
  if (input < 10) {
    //if the input is less than 10, prepend a '0' and return
    return '0'+input;
  }
  //otherwise return the input as a string; implicit "else" clause
  return input;
}
```

An important habit to get into, as early as possible, is to try and make your code as reusable as possible—or as dynamic as possible. Try to think of scenarios for which what you are currently doing could be used with minor modifications. For example, this method currently only works if your input number is under 100. Once you reach 100, your issue returns. We can update this method to easily work with any order of magnitude by adding an additional parameter which will specify how many digits we want the number to have—see Listing 6-4.

Listing 6-4. convertToIntegerString Method

```
/**
 * convertToIntegerString
 * @description Returns string representation of integers prepended by 0s
   based on desired magnitude
 * @param integer input
 * @aparam integer magnitude
 * @return string reprepsentation of integer
 */
```

```
public static string convertToIntegerString(integer input, integer magnitude){
  //convert the integer to a string
  string returnvalue = string.valueOf(input);

  /*if the string is shorter than desired length / magnitude, prepend a 0
    until it is*/
  while (returnValue.length()<magnitude){
    returnValue = '0'+returnValue;
  }

  //return the formatted string
  return returnValue;
}
```

Now we have two methods that can truly be considered to be utility methods and are worthy of being placed in the util.cls class. In order to use either the reverseList or convertToIntegerString methods from other classes, they can simply be called by util.reverseList(myListToReverse); and util.convertToIntegerString(myNumber, myDesiredMagnitude); respectively.

Note   Don't forget to capture the return values of your methods if there is one. Both of our utility methods return values which must be assigned to variables from the calling logic in order to be useful.

Method Reusability

Recall that methods are intended to be collections of statements which can be reused. We have already seen an example of what this looks like with the utility class methods in the previous section, but it is important to note that methods can call other methods; in fact, this is how complex logic is done. Take, for example, a method that is designed to calculate the difference, in business days only, between two dates. You could pass the result of this method into a method that then formats the result into a specific format. A common practice for utility methods is to create your own utility methods that simplify the number of parameters being passed through to already existing methods.

Consider the convertToIntegerString method. If your company only ever uses two-digit variations, it would be tiresome (and lower the readability of your code) to include the magnitude each time. It would make far more sense to include a rewritten version of our original twoDigitIntegerString method, which uses the covertToIntegerString method as in Listing 6-5.

Listing 6-5. Rewritten twoDigitIntegerString to Use covertToIntegerString

```
public static string twoDigitIntegerString(integer input){
  //return the return value of the convertToIntegerString
  // method with a prefilled magnitude
  return convertToIntegerString(input,2);
}
```

Object Class

At the heart of OOP is the type of class which represents a single object. These classes store attributes as well as methods specific to that object. Object classes can be created as stand-alone classes, complete with constructors, or they can be nested within other classes—commonly referred to as wrapper classes—and used to "wrap" a subset of attributes into an object class that is only relevant when used within the specific class (or context) where it appears.

A common example for using object classes on Force.com is to create representations of request and response objects from external services (covered in the *Salesforce Developer Pro* continuation). However, they can also be used to "wrap" together certain pieces of information in order to facilitate some other functionality. For example, let us assume we are building a custom Visualforce page that will allow us to select multiple Contact records. We would need to store a boolean attribute for selected. With that in mind, the following wrapper class in Listing 6-6 would ease our task.

Listing 6-6. Wrapper Class Example for Selecting Contact Records

```
public class contactWrapper{
  public Contact wrappedContactRecord;
  public boolean selected = false;
}
```

With this wrapper class in place, we can now instantiate a list collection of contactWrapper instead of Contacts: `list<ContactWrapper> myListOfContacts` rather than `list<Contact> myListOfContacts`. Again, remember that this contactWrapper class can be a stand-alone class, or nested within another class. It can also, but does not necessarily need to, have a constructor, or multiple overloaded constructors as in Listing 6-7.

Listing 6-7. contactWrapper class with Constructor Examples

```
/**
 * contactWrapper
 * @description class to contain a "selected" boolean matched to a specific
   Contact record
 */
public class contactWrapper{
  public Contact wrappedContactRecord;
  public boolean selected = false;

  //simple constructor to assign the contact
  public contactWrapper(Contact inputContact){
    wrappedContactRecord = inputContact;
  }

  //constructor to assign contact and selected boolean
  public contactWrapper(Contact inputContact, boolean inputBoolean){
    wrappedContactRecord = inputContact;
    selected = inputBoolean;
  }

  //default empty constructor, instantiates with a new blank Contact
  public contactWrapper(){
    wrappedContactRecord = new Contact();
  }
}
```

Now that we can instantiate new `contactWrappers`, it might make sense to include methods which will allow us to toggle the selected state. Let us add methods for select and deselect operations to the wrapper class as in Listing 6-8.

Listing 6-8. Select and Deselect Methods for the contactWrapper Class

```
//mark this wrapper as selected
public void select(){
  this.selected = true;
}

//mark this wrapper as deselected
public void deselect(){
  this.selected = false;
}

// can you tell what this does?
public void toggleSelectedState(){
  this.selected = (this.selected)?false:true;
}
```

In Listing 6-8, a third method called toggleSelectedState was added. Can you tell what it does? Using a ternary logic operator, it flips the value of selected. If it is currently selected, it deselects, and vice versa, which is akin to how checkboxes work. We will revisit our wrapper in the next chapter and put it to use with a Custom Apex Controller and some Visualforce.

Custom Apex Controllers

In Chapter 4, you were introduced to the Standard Controller and how it can be used to enabled data access and some minimal functionality on a Visualforce page. Using Apex, Custom Controllers can also be created, to be used in place of the Standard Controller. Controllers require a constructor method with no input parameters—see Listing 6-9.

Listing 6-9. Sample Custom Apex Controller with Constructor Method

```
//class definition
public class myCustomController{
  //constructor
    public myCustomController(){
  }
}
```

Like all other classes, Custom Controllers can contain attributes, nested wrapper classes, and custom methods. Custom Controllers can also be "extended" by extension classes.

Tip When working with Visualforce pages, there can only be one controller. You must make the determination whether your task is best served by using a standard controller, and possibly extending its functionality, or if it is better to start off by using a Custom Controller and build all of your required functionality from scratch.

Extensions

Extensions are another type of Apex Class. They are used to "extend" the functionality of controllers for use with Visualforce pages. Extensions can be used to extend both Standard Controllers (Listing 6-10) as well as Custom Controllers (Listing 6-11). Any class can be created as an extension or be "enabled" to be used as an extension by including a constructor with an input parameter of the controller to be extended as in Listing 6-12. We will cover extensions in more detail in the next chapter.

Listing 6-10. Standard Controller Extension

```
public class standardControllerExtension{
  /*standard controller extension by passing in the standard controller to
    constructor*/
  public standardControllerExtension(ApexPages.StandardController scon){
    //constructor logic here
  }
}
```

Listing 6-11. Custom Controller Extension

```
public class customControllerExtension{
  //custom controller extension by passing in a custom controller class to
    constructor
  public customControllerExtension(myCustomControllerClass ccon){
    //constructor logic here
  }
}
```

Listing 6-12. Nonextension Class Which Can Be Used as an Extension by Either Standard or Custom Controllers Thanks to Constructor Overloading

```
public class nonExtension{
  //standard controller extension constructor
  public nonExtension (ApexPages.StandardController scon){
    //constructor logic here
  }

  //custom controller extension constructor
  public nonExtension (myCustomControllerClass ccon){
    //constructor logic here
  }

  // other methods below
}
```

Warning   Remember, in order to use an extension, you must create a constructor within the extension class which requires the specific controller, either standard or specific custom class acting as a controller, as its input. This controller must be of the same type as the one in use by the Visualforce page on which you wish to use the extension class.

Triggers

Triggers are really Apex Classes, but they are a very special type of Apex class—they even get their own folder in the src folder! Database triggers, or triggers for short, are snippets of code which get run (execute) when a database operation occurs. These database operations should come naturally to you: insert, update, delete, undelete. This means that every time you create (insert) a new record, update a record, or delete or then undelete (restore) a record, a database trigger can be invoked.

Triggers for each of the database operations come in two distinct forms: a before trigger, and an after trigger. They are essentially the same, but behave very differently and there are some nuances to consider for each—and it is very important to know when to use which, and how.

Listing 6-13. Generic Trigger Class Definition Pseudocode

```
trigger triggerName on triggeringDatabaseObject
(commaSeparatedTriggeringActions){
  //trigger logic here
}
```

A single trigger can be created for multiple database events within a single trigger class (Listing 6-13). Trigger logic can then be filtered down by using special system methods on the trigger such as isBefore and isAfter or isInsert and isUpdate, which return booleans (true/false) and can be used in control logic statements (Listing 6-14).

Listing 6-14. Sample Trigger on Before and After Insert of Account

```
trigger myAccountTrigger on Account (before insert, after insert){
  if (trigger.isBefore && trigger.isInsert){
    //before insert logic here
  }

  if (trigger.isAfter && trigger.isInsert){
    //after insert logic here
  }
}
```

Warning   Triggers are inherently "bulkified." This means that a trigger will always execute on a list collection of 200 records (if at least 200 records are being manipulated). If more than 200 records are being manipulated, triggers automatically chunk into groups of 200 records at a time and process them as such. Keep this in mind as you write your trigger logic to ensure proper handling as well as to avoid governor limits.

There is some debate among the force.com developer community regarding the best structuring for trigger methods. Some argue that there should be a separate trigger class created for every database action, resulting in AccountBeforeInsert.trigger, AccountAfterInsert.trigger, AccountBeforeUpdate.trigger triggers and so forth. Although

this does keep the database events neatly distributed per object, many developers think that it generates too much file clutter to keep track of properly with larger databases (more objects).

Another part of the developer community opts for creating a single trigger class per object, AccountTrigger, for example, and containing all of the logic which determines which event occurred within the trigger class itself. This second group is then broken up into two further groups: those who put all of the application logic in the trigger as well, and those who simply use the trigger classes as routing classes based on triggering events to redirect to custom Apex classes which have methods for processing the data as needed. Ultimately, which design paradigm you choose for your trigger logic is entirely up to you; however, we will be covering the subject matter using trigger classes as routers to custom classes for handling our logic. Listings 6-15 through 6-17 show some examples of the various approaches to writing triggers.

Listing 6-15. Samples for Individual Trigger Classes for a Single Object

```
/**
* Account_beforeInsert.trigger
* @description Contains logic for beforeInsert trigger on Account
*/
trigger Account_beforeInsert on Account (before insert){
  for (Account a : trigger.new) {
    /* if there is an account name specified before insert, make sure it is
       capitalized.*/
    if (a.name != null) a.name = a.name.capitalize();
  }
}

/**
* Account_afterInsert.trigger
* @description Contains logic for afterInsert trigger on Account
*/
trigger Account_afterInsert on Account (after insert){
  for (Account a : trigger.new) {
    //do something for every Account record inserted.
  }
}
```

Tip   Remember, Account_beforeInsert.trigger and Account_afterInsert.trigger are separate trigger files! You must create two triggers if you opt for this design paradigm.

Listing 6-16. Sample for Trigger Classes with Routing and Processing Logic in Same Class

```
trigger AccountTrigger on Account (before insert, after insert){
  if (trigger.isBefore && trigger.isInsert){
    for (Account a : trigger.new){
      if (a.name != null) a.name = a.name.capitalize();
    }
  }
  else if( trigger.isAfter && trigger.isInsert){
    //after insert logic
  }
}
```

Listing 6-17. Sample for Trigger Classes with Routing to Apex Class Methods for Processing

```
/**
 * AccountTrigger.trigger
 * @description Trigger containing routing logic for Account object
 */
trigger AccountTrigger on Account (before insert, after insert){
  if (trigger.isBefore && trigger.isInsert){
    Account_Methods.beforeInsert(trigger.new);
  }
  else if( trigger.isAfter && trigger.isInsert){
    Account_Methods.afterInsert(trigger.new);
  }
}
```

```
/**
 * Account_Methods.cls
 * @description Class containing commonly used methods on the Account
   object
 */
public class Account_Methods{
  //handle trigger beforeInsert
  public static void beforeInsert(list<Account> newlist){
    for (Account a : trigger.new){
      if (a.name != null) a.name = a.name.capitalize();
    }
  }

  //handle trigger afterInsert
  public static void afterInsert(list<Account> newlist){
    //some after insert logic
  }
}
```

Looking at the preceding examples, you might be asking yourself why we would ever opt to use the last design paradigm (routing logic in trigger, processing in separate class). Keep in mind that the preceding examples are very short and succinct. When dealing with enterprise applications, it is not uncommon for hundreds of lines of code to be executed when a record is modified in the database. Keeping all of that logic within a single trigger file would be a nightmare to maintain (and likely hit the maximum class size restriction). By keeping all of the processing logic in a separate class (or classes), you also make it easier to construct test coverage to validate that your method is doing what is expected (covered in a later chapter), and there is also one other very important benefit to doing it this way. Triggers are special database classes, and as such, are locked and inaccessible, except by triggering a database event. Custom classes have no such restriction, which means that if you were to wish to execute the same logic on a record as if it were inserted to the database (without inserting it), you could. You would simply pass the object record to the Account_Methods.beforeInsert method (Listing 6-18)—but remember to include it in a list collection as the definition of the method stipulates.

Listing 6-18. Trigger Method Reusability Example

```
//create a new Account record named 'acme' and insert
Account account1 = new Account();
account1.name = 'acme';
insert account1;

/* Assuming the triggers from the prior sample executed without error,
 * this account's name would now be "Acme", and the Account would be
 * inserted into the database with a unique id.*/

//create a new Account record named 'acme' and mimic insert logic
Account account2 = new Account();
account2.name = 'acme';

/*we will need to create a list of Account to pass in as the parameter for
beforeInsert*/
list<Account> accountList = new list<Account>();

//add Account account2 to the list.
accountList.add(account2);

//call our processing function.
Account_Methods.beforeInsert(accountList);

/* accountListstill contains Account account2, with a capitalized name of
"Acme",
 * but Account account2 has not been inserted into the database,
 * and therefore has no id.*/
```

Hopefully, you can see how this starts bringing together all the concepts of modularity through classes and methods and enforces the reusability of code. This could be further optimized for reusability by creating a method in Account_Methods called formatName which could contain all the logic for when and how to modify an account's name. This method could then be called from anywhere to execute the logic of properly formatting an account's name. If the convention for naming new accounts ever changes, you would then only have to update the logic in one place. In the next sections, we will take a look at writing some actual trigger examples and see them in action in our instance.

Before we get there, however, there is one other topic that must be covered for everything to make sense. In the preceding examples, you may have noticed a reference to trigger.new. Since triggers operate on collections, we must have a way of retrieving the collection of records currently in scope. There are four different collections which triggers provide for this purpose.

- `Trigger.new (list<sObject>)` - a list collection of all records in this trigger context with their new values

- `Trigger.old (list<sObject>)` - a list collection of all records in this trigger context with their old values

- `Trigger.newMap (map<id, sObject>)` - a map collection of all records in this trigger context with their new values and mapped to their IDs

- `Trigger.oldMap (map<id, sObject>)` - a map collection of all records in this trigger context with their old values and mapped to their IDs

It is important to note that not every trigger has all of these collections available. In fact, only the update trigger has all four available. Insert triggers only have `trigger.new`. They do not have `trigger.newmap` because the records do not have an ID to map to. Insert triggers also do not have either `trigger.old` or `trigger.oldMap` because these are new records—there are no old values. Delete and undelete triggers have only the old values available and therefore only `trigger.old` and `trigger.oldmap`. Note, however, that after a deletion takes place, `trigger.oldmap` becomes limited in usefulness as the IDs mapped for the records no longer exist in the database. The undelete trigger is also very specific and nuanced and is therefore not commonly used by beginners. As mentioned, the update trigger has access to all four collections, and the respective values can be used in a variety of ways to compare the records being updated against their previous values.

Insert Triggers

Insert triggers, as the name implies, are triggered when a record is inserted (created) into the database. An important note here is that until the thread finishes execution, the record does not exist in the database (it is not committed), and therefore has no unique ID—this is the before insert trigger stage. Once the before insert trigger has completed,

in the same thread, the after insert trigger begins executing. The after insert trigger does have a unique ID, as the record has been inserted into the database, but if a fatal error occurs before the thread completes, the entire thread is rolled back and the record is never committed to the database.

Before Insert Triggers

A common use case for before insert triggers is if the business would like to format data entry fields or pull in additional information to automate the population of certain fields. An easy example of this is to capitalize Contact first and last names to standardize the names when dealing with users who might type them in lowercase. We will need to create a trigger and class for this.

Let us start by creating the class and our method to house the logic for use by the trigger. Using your IDE of choice, create a new class and name it Contact_Methods, indicating that methods contained in this class relate to the Contact object. If you are using the Developer Console, follow the instructions for creating the Util class from earlier in this chapter. For Eclipse, right-click the src folder and select "New" and then "Apex Class" as in Figure 6-5. For SublimeText with MavensMate, select MavensMate from the menu, then "Metadata", and finally "New Apex Class" as in Figure 6-6. In all scenarios, you will be prompted to provide the name of the class "Contact_Methods".

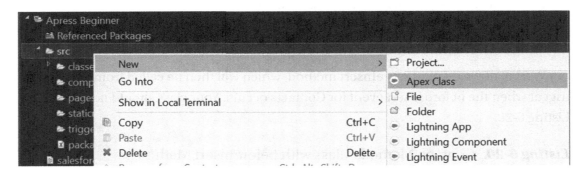

Figure 6-5. *Eclipse IDE Apex Class creation*

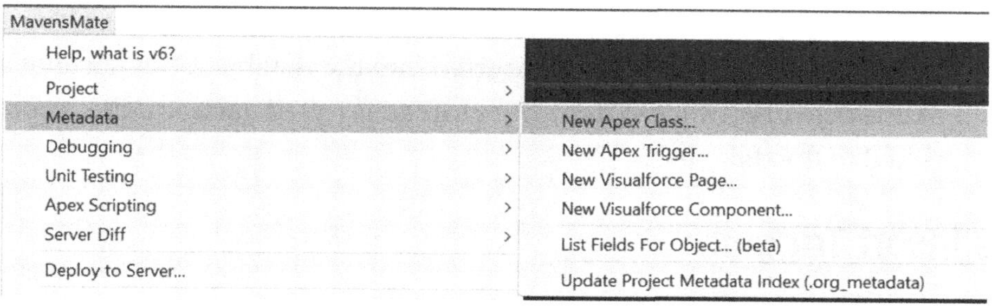

Figure 6-6. *SublimeText with MavensMate Apex Class creation*

Note   Depending on the version and configuration of MavensMate you are using, you may also be prompted to select a template. Selecting the default template will work for our purposes.

You should now see a class called Contact_Methods. Depending on which IDE you used, you may or may not have a constructor method included—which you should delete. Your class should have the code in Listing 6-19 only at this point.

Listing 6-19. Starting Contact_Methods Code

```
public with sharing class Contact_Methods {

}
```

We will now add our beforeInsert method, which will then be called from the trigger when the before insert event for Contacts occurs. Your class should now look like Listing 6-20.

Listing 6-20. Contact_Methods Class with beforeInsert Method

```
/**
 * Contact_Methods
 * @description A collection of methods pertaining to the Contact object
 */
public with sharing class Contact_Methods {
  /**
   * beforeInsert
```

```
 * @description A static method for the Contact object containing
 * logic to be performed on the before insert event.
 * @param newlist List collection of Contact records to execute logic on
 */
public static void beforeInsert(list<Contact> newlist){

  //for every Contact record in the passed collection
  for (Contact c : newlist){

    //check if firstName is not blank before operating on it
    if (String.isNotBlank(c.firstName)){
      c.firstName = c.firstName.capitalize();
    }

    //check if lastName is not blank before operating on it
    if (String.isNotBlank(c.lastName)){
      c.lastName = c.lastName.capitalize();
    }
  }
}
}
```

Warning   Whenever operating on a value, you should always check to ensure that it is not null to avoid null pointer exceptions and fatal errors.

Now, we need the trigger to call this method. Similar to creating a new class, open the corresponding menu in your IDE of choice, but this time select "New Apex Trigger" rather than "New Apex Class" and name the trigger Contact_Trigger. Depending on your IDE, you will be presented with a different way of selecting the trigger object. In Eclipse, this is a drop-down. In SublimeText, you specify the class name, followed by a comma, and finally the object name: `Contact_Trigger, Contact` as seen in Figure 6-7. Your IDE will also determine how you select the events; this is largely unimportant for our purposes, as you can add events later by altering the code of the class. Whatever your IDE's default is will be suitable.

```
Apex Trigger API Name, Object API Name Contact_Trigger, Contact
```

Figure 6-7. *SublimeText with MavensMate new trigger creation*

We will use this trigger to route to our beforeInsert method in the Contact_Methods class. Your code should look as Listing 6-21.

Listing 6-21. Contact_Trigger with beforeInsert Event Routed to Contact_Methods

```
trigger Contact_Trigger on Contact (before insert) {

  //route before insert event to corresponding Contact_Methods method
  if(trigger.isBefore && trigger.isInsert){
    Contact_Methods.beforeInsert(trigger.new);
  }
}
```

Let's test this out. If we try to create a new Contact now, and type their name in lowercase, the trigger will correct this data for us and insert the Contact with properly capitalized names. See Figure 6-8 and Figure 6-9.

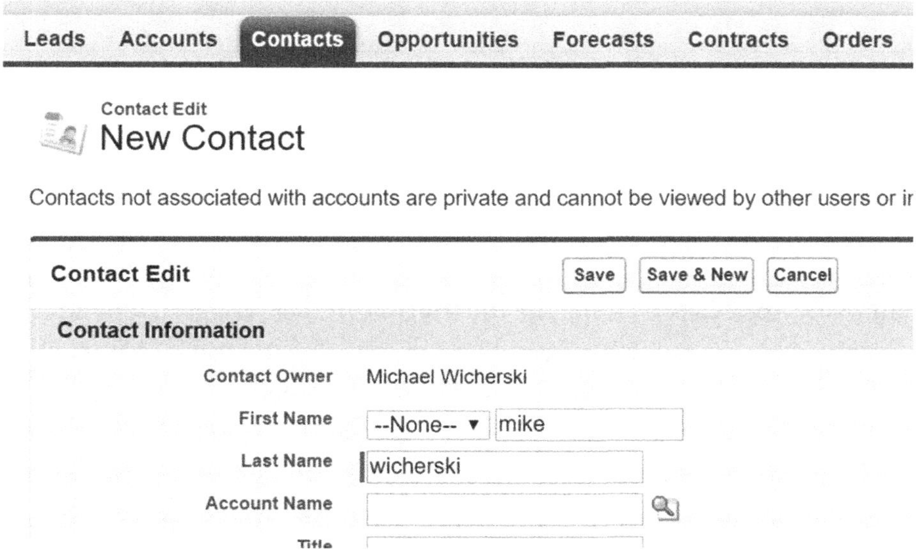

Figure 6-8. *Creating a new Contact with lowercase name*

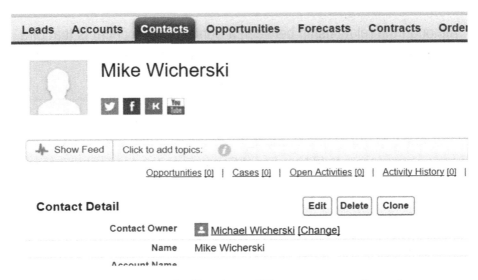

Figure 6-9. *Trigger correct capitalization of Contact name from lowercase*

Our insert trigger worked and did its job. We can see that the name is properly capitalized; but what if I were to edit it back to a lowercase? Since our trigger is only on before insert, I can update the record to be lowercase without any trouble. This is probably undesired, and we will see how to tackle it in the update trigger section. For now, let us move on to after insert.

Note   You could also manually call Contact_Methods.beforeInsert on a list collection with just this one Contact record to execute the logic, demonstrating the benefit of structuring triggers and classes in this manner.

After Insert Triggers

A common after insert trigger is to perform some additional processing on related records, or perhaps integrations with external systems (covered in the *Salesforce Developer Pro* title). A good example would be to perform the same funtionality as a roll-up summary field on lookup relationships rather than master-details; for example, to calculate the number of Contacts related to a given Account.

Note Although the relationship between a Contact and Account is that of a Master-Detail, with the Contact being the child, Roll-up summary fields are not available. This is a special case.

For this example, we will need to create a new field on the Account object and update our Contact_Methods and Contact_Trigger class and trigger, respectively. Let's start by creating our custom field Number of Contacts on the Account object.

1. Click Setup

2. Navigate to Customize

3. Navigate to Accounts

4. Navigate to Fields

5. Select "New" next to Account Custom Fields and Relationships (Figure 6-10)

Figure 6-10. *Creating a new Account field*

6. Follow the prompts for creating a new number field, with 0 decimal places called "Number of Contacts" (select the default for all sharing/layout options)

7. You should now see something similar to Figure 6-11, with the Number of Contacts field created.

Account Custom Fields & Relationships		New Field Dependencies	
Action	**Field Label**	**API Name**	**Data Type**
Edit | Del | Replace	Active	Active__c	Picklist
Edit | Del | Replace	Customer Priority	CustomerPriority__c	Picklist
Edit | Del	Number of Contacts	Number_of_Contacts__c	Number(18, 0)
Edit | Del	Number of Locations	NumberofLocations__c	Number(3, 0)
Edit | Del | Replace	SLA	SLA__c	Picklist
Edit | Del	SLA Expiration Date	SLAExpirationDate__c	Date
Edit | Del	SLA Serial Number	SLASerialNumber__c	Text(10)
Edit | Del | Replace	Upsell Opportunity	UpsellOpportunity__c	Picklist

Figure 6-11. *Number of Contacts field created on Account*

Note the API name of our new field, and let us create the afterInsert method now in Contact_Methods to populate this field (Listing 6-22).

Listing 6-22. afterInsert Method of Contact_Methods Class

```
/**
 * afterInsert
 * @description A static method for the Contact object containing
 * logic to be performed on the after insert event
 * @param newlist List collection of Contact records to execute logic on
 */
public static void afterInsert(list<Contact> newlist){

  //set collection of related accountIds from Contacts
  set<id> accountIds = new set<id>();

  for (Contact c : newlist){

    //if this Contact record has a related Account, store the Account's id
    if (c.accountId != null){
      accountIds.add(c.accountId);
    }
  }
```

```
//perform aggregate query to count the number of Contacts for each account
//affected by this trigger event
//ContactCount will be the alias for the aggregate count of Contacts
//This aggregate query will be grouped by the AccountId
list<AggregateResult> accountContactsAggregate = [select
                                                  accountId,
                                                  count(id) ContactCount
                                                  from Contact
                                                  where accountId IN
                                                    :accountIds
                                                  group by accountId];

//create a list collection of Accounts which will require updates
list <Account> accountsToUpdate = new list<Account>();

//for each aggregate result, representing an Account,
//set the Number of Contacts field
for (AggregateResult ar : accountContactsAggregate){

  //create a representation of our Account with the given id
  Account currentAccount = new
  Account(id=string.valueOf(ar.get('accountId')));

  //set the Number of Contacts field from the aggregate result
  currentAccount.Number_of_Contacts__c = integer.valueOf(ar.
  get('ContactCount'));

  //add the account to the update collection
   accountsToUpdate.add(currentAccount);
}

//perform the database update of affected Accounts
update accountsToUpdate;
}
```

Warning   Do not forget to update your trigger class (Listing 6-23) to handle and route the new trigger event! It is one of the most common mistakes made, even for veterans.

Listing 6-23. Updated Contact_Trigger with After Insert Event

```
trigger Contact_Trigger on Contact (before insert, after insert) {

  //route before insert event to corresponding Contact_Methods method
  if(trigger.isBefore && trigger.isInsert){
    Contact_Methods.beforeInsert(trigger.new);
  }

  //route after insert event to corresponding Contact_Methods method
  if(trigger.isAfter && trigger.isInsert){
    Contact_Methods.afterInsert(trigger.new);
  }
```

Let's see how this works by creating a few Contacts on our "My First Account" Account. Your layout will likely look different from the following screenshots; I have modified the layout to make the Number of Contacts more prominent in the right column to make it easier to find. In Figure 6-12 you can see that the field is blank, which is the default value for that field. If we click New Contact in the Contacts section, create a new Contact, and then come back to this Account, we will see that it now has a value of 1 as in Figure 6-13.

Figure 6-12. *Account with no Contacts*

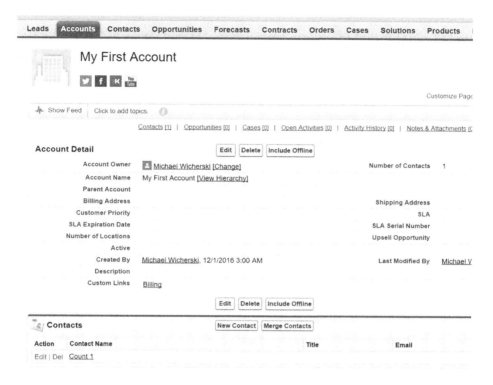

Figure 6-13. *Account with one Contact*

Can you spot a problem yet? What happens if we delete this Contact? Or, what happens if we change this Contact's related Account or change another Contact's account to be this account? Currently, only the creation of a new contact directly on this account from the start modifies our Number of Contacts field, which will lead to this field being out of date very quickly. Let us see how we can leverage the other triggers to bring this functionality full circle and optimize some of our code while we are at it.

Update

We have already found a few instances where we would like to have the same logic executed on update events as we did for insert events. We can use the update triggers to call our existing methods since the logic to execute is the same, but that is not best practice and it is absolutely horrible for scaling. Instead, let us refactor our code. Refactoring is the process of taking existing code and rewriting it in order to optimize or structure it better for the purposes of improved readability, efficiency, and scalability without changing its actual functionality (Listing 6-24).

Listing 6-24. Refactored Contact_Methods

```
/**
 * Contact_Methods
 * @description A collection of methods pertaining to the Contact object
 */
public with sharing class Contact_Methods {

  /**
   * beforeInsert
   * @description A static method for the Contact object containing
   * logic to be performed on the before insert event.
   * @param newlist List collection of Contact records to execute logic on
   */

  public static void beforeInsert(list<Contact> newlist){

    //for every Contact record in the passed collection
    for (Contact c : newlist){
      formatContactName(c);
    }
  }

  /**
   * afterInsert
   * @description A static method for the Contact object containing
   * logic to be performed on the after insert event
   * @param newlist List collection of Contact records to execute logic on
   */
  public static void afterInsert(list<Contact> newlist){

    //retrieve set of Account Ids for these Contacts and update Account Number
    // of Contacts field where applicable
    updateAccountNumberOfContacts(retrieveSetOfContactAccounts(newlist));
  }
```

```
/**
 * formatContactName
 * @description Utility method for formatting a Contact's first and
 *    last name to be uppercase
 * @param  input A Contact record
 */
static void formatContactName(Contact input){
  //check if firstName is not blank before operating on it
  if (String.isNotBlank(input.firstName)){
    input.firstName = input.firstName.capitalize();
  }

  //check if lastName is not blank before operating on it
  if (String.isNotBlank(input.lastName)){
    input.lastName = input.lastName.capitalize();
  }
}

/**
 * retrieveSetOfContactAccounts
 * @description Utility method to retrieve a set of related Account ids
 *    given a collection of Contacts
 * @param  contacts List collection of Contact records to extract Account
   ids from
 */
public static set<id> retrieveSetOfContactAccounts(list<Contact> contacts){

  //set collection of related accountIds from Contacts
  set<id> accountIds = new set<id>();

  for (Contact c : contacts){

    //if this Contact record has a related Account, store the Account's id
    if (c.accountId != null){
      accountIds.add(c.accountId);
    }
  }
```

```
  //return set of Account Ids
  return accountIds;
}

/**
 * updateAccountNumberOfContacts
 * @description A static method used to update the Number of Contacts
   field for
 * related accounts determined by the passed in collection of Account Ids
 * @param  accountIds Set collection of accountIds
 */
public static void updateAccountNumberOfContacts(set<id> accountIds){
  //perform aggregate query to count the number of Contacts for each account
  // affected by this trigger event
  // ContactCount will be the alias for the aggregate count of Contacts
  // This aggregate query will be grouped by the AccountId
  List<AggregateResult> accountContactsAggregate = [select accountId,
  count(id) ContactCount
    from Contact where accountId IN :accountIds group by accountId];

  //create a list collection of Accounts which will require updates
  list<Account> accountsToUpdate = new list<Account>();

  /*for each aggregate result, representing an Account, set the Number of
  Contacts field*/
  for (AggregateResult ar : accountContactsAggregate){

    //create a representation of our Account with the given id
    Account currentAccount = new Account(id=string.valueOf(ar.
    get('accountId')));

    //set the Number of Contacts field from the aggregate result
    currentAccount.Number_of_Contacts__c = integer.valueOf(ar.
    get('ContactCount'));

    //add the account to the update collection
    accountsToUpdate.add(currentAccount);
  }
```

```
    //perform the database update of affected Accounts
    update accountsToUpdate;
  }
}
```

Notice how every action has been moved into its own, very specific method. Every piece can now be independently called, by as many things as need it. The functionality is no longer bound to only trigger actions. This is the essence of the modular programming paradigm, as you want your code to always be as reusable as possible. Adding the desired functionality to an update trigger event now is simply a matter of creating the routing handler for it as in Listing 6-25.

Listing 6-25. Contact_Methods beforeUpdate Method

```
/**
 * beforeUpdate
 * @description A static method for the Contact object containing
 * logic to be performed on the before update event.
 * @param newlist List collection of Contact records to execute logic on
 */

public static void beforeUpdate(list<Contact> newlist, list<Contact>
oldList){

  //for every Contact record in the passed collection
  for (Contact c : newlist){
    formatContactName(c);
  }
}
```

Keep in mind that you can often optimize your execution time in update triggers by considering what is happening, and evaluating whether or not certain branches of logic should be executed. In this instance, for example, we would only really have to format the Contact name if it was different in the new version than it was in the old version; otherwise, it would already have been formatted (assuming of course there was no data entry prior to the insert trigger being put in place). This means that we can improve our update method by building on the insert method and adding a condition as in Listing 6-26.

Listing 6-26. Contact_Methods beforeUpdate Method with Conditional for Name Formatting

```
/**
 * beforeUpdate
 * @description A static method for the Contact object containing
 * logic to be performed on the before update event.
 * @param newlist List collection of Contact records to execute logic on
 */

public static void beforeUpdate(list<Contact> newlist, list<Contact> oldList){

  //for every Contact record in the passed collection
  for (integer i=0; i <newlist.size(); i++){
    //if first or last name has changed only
    if (newList[i].firstName != oldList[i].firstName ||
          newList[i].lastName != oldList[i].lastName){
      formatContactName(newlist[i]);
    }
  }
}
```

Notice that instead of using the for sObject in the collection format of the for loop, we are using the incremental integer style. Collections passed through a trigger are always in the same order, which means that the first element in the new collection will always correspond to the first element in the old collection, which allows us to very quickly compare the two versions without figuring out a way to map them against each other.

Tip   Trigger collections are always passed in the same order. This is specifically useful when dealing with update triggers and comparing old vs. new collections of elements, as they will always be at the same index of their respective collection.

As for our afterUpdate method in Listing 6-27 in Contact_Methods (and related trigger in Listing 6-28), it will have identical elements to our insert method, which brings up a special case where upsert trigger methods come into play—covered next. Note that our update method also calls the updateAccountNumberOfContacts method on the

oldList. This is because if a Contact was moved from one account to another, we need to update the old account's number of contacts as well as the new account's. Note that this could be further optimized by refactoring the code to include a set collection that stores all the retrieved IDs of both old and new accounts and calls the method only once. Since sets automatically maintain unique values, there is no risk of duplicate entries. However, for the purposes of this example and subsequent upsert trigger examples, we will allow the code to be a little unoptimized—in the name of science.

Listing 6-27. Contact_Methods afterUpdate Method

```
/**
 * afterUpdate
 * @description A static method for the Contact object containing
 * logic to be performed on the after update event
 * @param newlist List collection of Contact records to execute logic on
 */
public static void afterUpdate(list<Contact> newlist, list<Contact> oldList){

  //retrieve set of Account Ids for these Contacts and update Account
  // Number of Contacts field where applicable
  updateAccountNumberOfContacts(retrieveSetOfContactAccounts(newlist));
  updateAccountNumberOfContacts(retrieveSetOfContactAccounts(oldlist));
}
```

Listing 6-28. Contact_Trigger with Update Events

```
trigger Contact_Trigger on Contact (before insert, after insert, before
update, after update) {

        //route before insert event to corresponding Contact_Methods method
        if(trigger.isBefore && trigger.isInsert){
                Contact_Methods.beforeInsert(trigger.new);
        }

        //route after insert event to corresponding Contact_Methods method
        if(trigger.isAfter && trigger.isInsert){
                Contact_Methods.afterInsert(trigger.new);
        }
```

```
    //route before update event to corresponding Contact_Methods method
    if (trigger.isBefore && trigger.isUpdate){
        contact_Methods.beforeUpdate(trigger.new, trigger.old);
    }

    //route after update event to corresponding Contact_Methods method
    if (trigger.isAfter && trigger.isUpdate){
        Contact_Methods.afterUpdate(trigger.new, trigger.old);
    }
}
```

Upsert

An Upsert trigger (Listing 6-30) does not strictly exist. It is a nomenclature used by developers to describe logic which is executed on both Insert and Update triggers, and can be applied to both before as well as after trigger scenarios. From our preceding examples, it is likely that we want to enforce our naming of Contacts always. If a user goes in and updates the first name, and types it in all in lowercase again, we would want our trigger to run and capitalize that name again before saving the updated record. If we are counting Contacts related to an Account only if specific criteria are met, it is important for us to check whether or not data has been updated to now meet, or conversely, fail to meet, those criteria.

In our update trigger section, we modified our beforeUpdate method to have additional logic controlling whether or not to execute the formatting of a Contact's name. However, our after update logic had portions identical to our after insert logic, which initiated the calculation of the number of contacts on an Account. In this scenario, we could use an afterUpsert trigger method (Listing 6-29) to facilitate the common actions, which will replace the entirety of the afterInsert method logic and trim the afterUpdate method.

Listing 6-29. Renamed afterInsert Method to afterUpsert

```
/**
 * afterUpsert
 * @description A static method for the Contact object containing
 * logic to be performed on the after insert and update event
 * @param newlist List collection of Contact records to execute logic on
```

```
 */
public static void afterUpsert(list<Contact> newlist){

  //retrieve set of Account Ids for these Contacts and update Account Number
  // of Contacts field where applicable
  updateAccountNumberOfContacts(retrieveSetOfContactAccounts(newlist));
}
```

Listing 6-30. Contact_Trigger Updated with afterUpsert Routing in Place of afterInsert

```
trigger Contact_Trigger on Contact (before insert, after insert, before
update, after update) {

  //route before insert event to corresponding Contact_Methods method
  if(trigger.isBefore && trigger.isInsert){
    Contact_Methods.beforeInsert(trigger.new);
  }

  //route after insert and update events to corresponding Contact_Methods method
  if(trigger.isAfter && (trigger.isInsert || trigger.isUpdate)){
    Contact_Methods.afterUpsert(trigger.new);
  }

  //route before update event to corresponding Contact_Methods method
  if (trigger.isBefore && trigger.isUpdate){
    contact_Methods.beforeUpdate(trigger.new, trigger.old);
  }

  //route after update event to corresponding Contact_Methods method
  if (trigger.isAfter && trigger.isUpdate){
    Contact_Methods.afterUpdate(trigger.new, trigger.old);
  }
}
```

Tip   Although it is perfectly acceptable to route to the insert and update methods already established from your upsert triggers, it provides far greater granular control to create a new upsert method to handle these situations, allowing you to keep insert-only and update-only actions separate more easily.

Delete and Undelete

Deletion triggers (Listing 6-31) are typically used to process actions on related records/notify external systems rather than on the triggering record itself: after all, it's being deleted. Undelete triggers have many quirks, and their implementation is not typically seen except in very advanced business applications, so we will leave them for later. However, even in our example use case, we can make some limited use of them. We need to calculate the change in Number of Contacts on an Account when a Contact is deleted, as well as when it is undeleted. Luckily, this is very similar to our upsert methodology, where our logic is identical for both: we just need to call the calculation method.

In this scenario, rather than creating new methods in Contact_Methods to handle our trigger, let us call the calculcation method directly from the trigger class. There is nothing preventing you from creating handler methods in Contact_Methods; in fact, that would be preferred in order to remain consistent, but the goal here is to demonstrate the versatility of Apex structuring and to expose you to multiple different ways in which you can do so. It is also another example of how to call methods across classes—just remember your access modifiers, public, in this case.

Listing 6-31. Deletion triggers

```
trigger Contact_Trigger on Contact (before insert, after insert,
  before update, after update, after delete) {

  //route before insert event to corresponding Contact_Methods method
  if(trigger.isBefore && trigger.isInsert){
    Contact_Methods.beforeInsert(trigger.new);
  }
```

```
  /*route after insert and update events to corresponding Contact_Methods
method*/
  if(trigger.isAfter && (trigger.isInsert || trigger.isUpdate)){
    Contact_Methods.afterUpsert(trigger.new);
  }

  //route before update event to corresponding Contact_Methods method
  if (trigger.isBefore && trigger.isUpdate){
    contact_Methods.beforeUpdate(trigger.new, trigger.old);
  }

  //route after update event to corresponding Contact_Methods method
  if (trigger.isAfter && trigger.isUpdate){
    Contact_Methods.afterUpdate(trigger.new, trigger.old);
  }

  //handle deletion and undeletion directly
  if (trigger.isAfter && (trigger.isDelete || trigger.isUndelete)){
    // note the line break in the method parameter for formatting purposes
    Contact_Methods.updateAccountNumberOfContacts(
      Contact_Methods.retrieveSetOfContactAccounts(trigger.old)
    );
  }
}
```

Trigger Chains

A topic so important, albeit short, that it gets its own breakout section! You have already seen how to create triggers for Accounts and Contacts, but what if you create both? What if your Contact trigger causes the Account update trigger to be executed? Which then causes your Contact update trigger to run, which again causes your Account trigger to run? Well, you end up with an endless loop, and eventually you will hit a max trigger-depth exception from a governor limit and the entire thread will be rolled back with an error. Needless to say, this is bad. Very bad. So what can you do to prevent this? After all, there may be situations where you actually want to have a Contact event trigger an update to an Account, and then update the contact one more time. This is where

static booleans come into play, and you can use them to construct flow controls with criteria to allow the trigger chain to execute only as many times as you want. The most common implementation of this is to have a boolean called `beforeInsertHasRun` for example, which gets set to true as soon as the trigger begins execution. Then, in your logic, your flow control would simply be if (`!beforeInsertHasrun`), allowing your logic to execute only if that trigger event has not already been processed and skip over the logic otherwise through to completion of the thread.

Summary

This chapter has exposed you to actually writing Apex with what you have learned in Chapter 5. The ability to write Apex classes and triggers is at the very heart of a Salesforce developer's toolkit as it allows you to turn your company's business logic into programmatic statements which can enforce your requirements and help maintain clean data, as well as help automate tasks. We even saw some data crunching with the Number of Contacts which can generate new data useful to your users.

In the next chapter, we will take what you have learned about Visualforce and slam it together with what you have learned about Apex thus far in order to create intelligent Visualforce pages. By using Apex controllers and extensions to enhance your Visualforce pages, you can create interfaces that can aid your users in their productivity.

CHAPTER 7

Visualforce with Apex

Salesforce is great out of the box. It has a truckload of baked-in goodies and features to hit the ground running with, and it is fairly customizable for administrators to declaratively tailor the application to the organization's needs. As a developer, however, it is your charge to take everything to the next level and improve on the user experience, building on top of what Salesforce already provides. One of the most common complaints from users, once the hype of having a new system wears off, is that managing the data in Salesforce becomes very click-intensive (not to mention spread across many different pages, and their associated load times). In this chapter, we are going to take a look at how we can use the knowledge about Visualforce from Chapter 4, and Apex from Chapters 5 and 6, to create custom interfaces to help streamline the user experience and make employees happier and more productive.

Throughout the chapter, we will step through creating a Contact management interface to aid the user in managing multiple Contacts on their respective Accounts. We will start slow, with a basic page, and progress toward an increasingly complex and interactive page. By the end of this chapter, you will be able to write a custom Visualforce page, with Apex-driven logic that is applicable to a real-world use case.

This feels more like a Coca Cola, or Pepsi if that's your preference, type of chapter. There will be plenty of examples and pictures, but sadly still no pop-up images though.

Custom Controllers

We are going to approach this topic backward from Salesforce's point of view. Typically, you would first learn how to extend a Standard Controller with an Extension Apex Class, and then venture on to create your own stand-alone Custom Controller Apex Class. However, with this approach, we will see and truly appreciate the functionality that a Standard Controller provides you with—but you will also know how it all works under the hood and be able to replicate it from scratch in case you ever want to tweak certain aspects.

© Michael Wicherski 2017
M. Wicherski, *Beginning Salesforce Developer*, https://doi.org/10.1007/978-1-4842-3300-9_7

So, then, what are Custom Controllers? Custom Controllers are simply Apex Classes which expose their methods and/or variables to a Visualforce page. In order to do this, these classes must have a constructor method, and all methods and variables must be publicly exposed (using the public access modifier). Custom Controllers respect the with and without sharing security definitions you learned about in Chapter 6.

Note   Custom Controllers are Apex Classes which require a constructor method and follow the with sharing/without sharing security model.

Account Manager

For the use case we will be solving throughout this chapter, we will mainly be working with two files, an Apex Class containing our Custom Controller, and a Visualforce page which will utilize the controller. In the Standard Controller Extension section, we will add a second Visualforce page which will utilize our controller as an Extension instead—with some modifications to the controller, of course.

As has been mentioned before, there are many different ways of doing things on the Force.com platform. Let us take a walk on the wild side for a moment and do something no (or at least hardly any) developer would ever really do: create an Apex class in the browser. To do this, follow the steps in Figure 7-1.

1. Click Setup

2. Navigate to the Develop section under Build and expand it

3. Click Apex Classes

4. Click New

Figure 7-1.   *Creating Apex Class via browser*

Once you do this, you should see a page similar to the one in Figure 7-2. Add the following code from Listing 7-1, then save this file as Account_Manager, and let us get out of here and back into a proper developer environment.

Figure 7-2. *New Apex Class edit screen as seen in browser*

Listing 7-1. Account_Manager Apex Class Starting Code

```
public with sharing class Account_Manager {
  public Account_Manager(){
  }
}
```

Tip   Notice that by specifying the class name in your class body (code), the filename was set for you when you hit Save.

Caution   Refreshing from the server overrides your local copy of any files retrieved from the server. If you have pending work that has not been uploaded to the server, make sure you save a copy to avoid losing it.

You may notice that if you now switch back to your IDE, it does not have your Account_Methods class as in Figure 7-3. This is normal. After all, your IDE is working off of the local files on your computer, and at this point, it is out of sync with the Force. com servers, since changes were made directly on the server via the browser. It's easy to correct this; simply right-click your project and select the "Refresh from server" option as seen in Figure 7-4. You will be prompted to confirm that you wish to overwrite your local files—you will lose any pending work if your files are different in any way from the server's copy. Once the operation completes, you should see your Account_Manager.cls file under the classes folder of your project with the generic code you saved in it (see Figure 7-5).

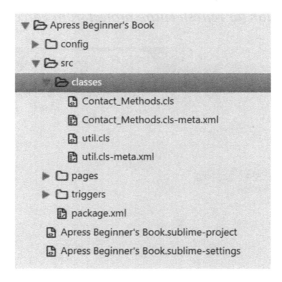

Figure 7-3. *Missing Account_Methods class from local IDE*

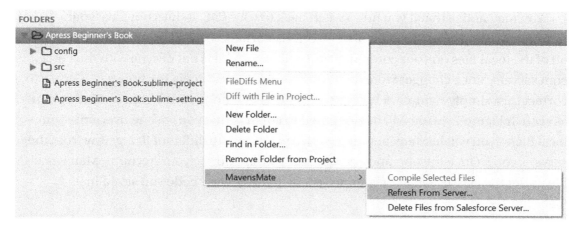

Figure 7-4. *Menu option for refresh entire project from Force.com servers*

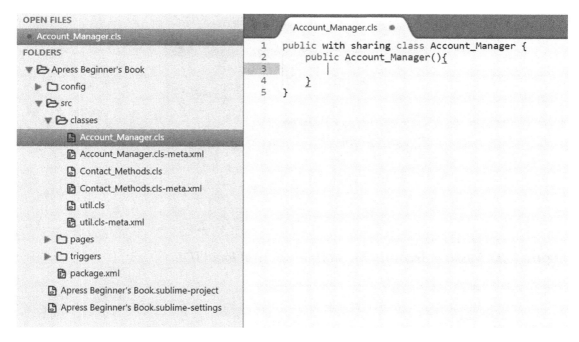

Figure 7-5. *Refreshed local copies with Account_Manager class now available*

Note   Depending on which IDE you are using, your menu options might be slightly different. Look for your IDE plug-in's name (such as MavensMate), or for Force.com / Salesforce. The refresh from server option should be the same across them all once you find the correct parent menu.

Tip   You might be able to save some time on larger projects if you sync only the folder/specific file (if you have it already).

While we are at it, let us also create the corresponding Visualforce page we are going to use and call it Account_Manager as well. How you create this page is up to you at this point. You can do so via the browser setup area, the Developer Console, or your IDE. In order to reinforce the concept of local files syncing with the server, I would suggest doing it this time via the browser:

1.   Click Setup

2.   Navigate to Develop under the Build section

3.   Click Visualforce Pages

4.   Click New

Feel free to delete everything between the opening and closing <apex:page> tags before saving as in Figure 7-6.

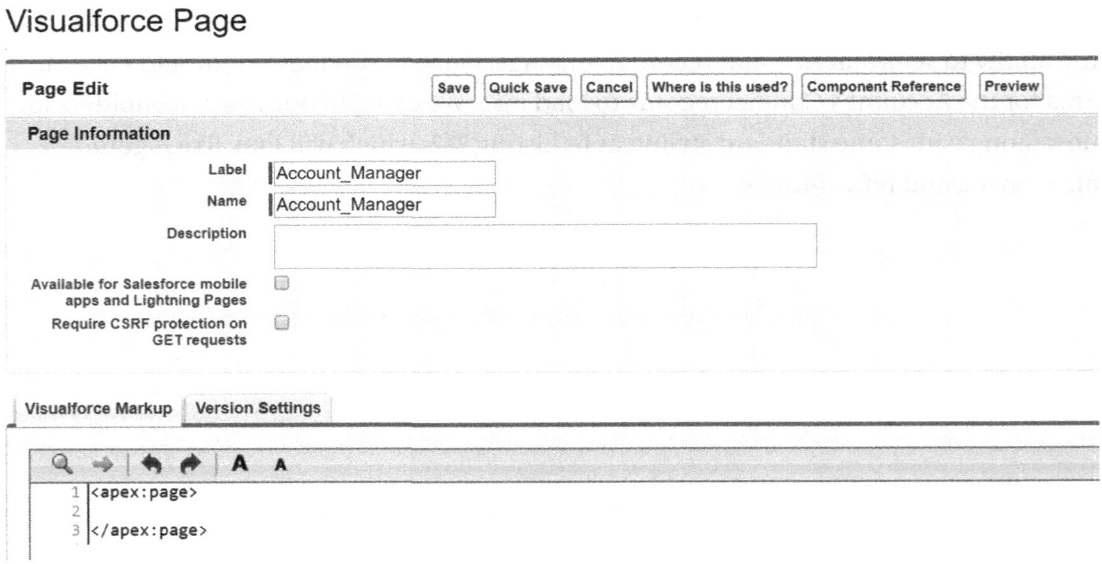

Visualforce Page

Page Edit	Save	Quick Save	Cancel	Where is this used?	Component Reference	Preview

Page Information

Label	Account_Manager
Name	Account_Manager
Description	
Available for Salesforce mobile apps and Lightning Pages	☐
Require CSRF protection on GET requests	☐

Visualforce Markup | **Version Settings**

```
1  <apex:page>
2
3  </apex:page>
```

Figure 7-6. *New Account_Manager page created via browser setup*

181

Tip   Remember to refresh your local files; try just refreshing the pages folder this time around.

So now we should have both of our files ready to go in our local IDE, Account_Manager. cls and Account_Manager.page, so let us get started. Since we do not have a project plan, or any real specifications or documentation for this project, we are going to approach it iteratively, meaning we will keep going back and improving on it step by step, building and refining our functionality as needed. First off, let us open the page in our browser so we can see our progress as we go. Since we have not made a button or any other way to access this page yet, simply modify the URL while logged in.

You can navigate to any custom Visualforce page in the system by modifying the URL after the .com portion. By adding /apex/<pagename>, where <pagename> should be replaced by the name of your page, the system will automatically redirect you to the correct location. In our case, we should be navigating to .com/apex/Account_Manager (my specific URL right now is https://na35.salesforce.com/apex/Account_Manager). You should see an amazingly boring blank page, which is reflective of our intricately coded <apex:page> </apex:page> page thus far.

Let us flesh this page out a bit more. At a minimum, we are going to need an area and the ability to select an Account record to manage. Once we do that, we should have an area for the Account's Contact records to load into. We can add both as placeholders for now along with some standard styling as in Listing 7-2, which will look like Figure 7-7 after saving and refreshing.

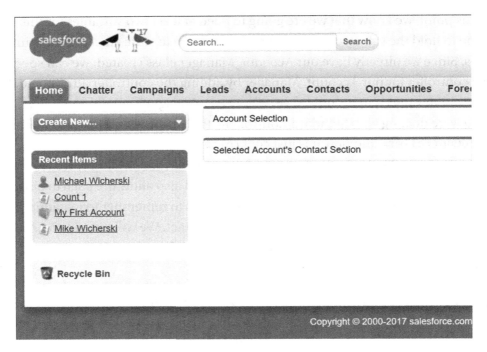

Figure 7-7. *Starting Account_Manager page*

Listing 7-2. Beginning Structure for Account_Manager page

```
<apex :page showHeader="true" sidebar="true">
  <apex:pageBlock>
    Account Selection
  </apex:pageBlock>
  <apex:pageBlock>
    Selected Account's Contact Section
  </apex:pageBlock>
</apex:page>
```

Tip Using the URL structure trick, you can also easily distinguish when you are viewing a custom page. Standard pages will never have the apex keyword in the URL.

At this point, we know that we are going to need at least two variables for this page: one to hold the selected Account, and a collection to store all of that Account's Contacts. Since we already have our Account_Manager class created, we can specify it as the controller for our Account_Manager by adding the controller attribute to the page definition `<apex:page controller="Account_Manager" ... >`. Notice that when we were dealing with Standard Controllers, the attribute on the page tag was `standardController=` and now it is just `controller=`.

In our Account_Method class, let us add the variables we now know we will need as in Listing 7-3. Remember to make them public, and also allow the page to both set their values as well as get them. Also very important is to remember to instantiate and initialize our collection variable and placeholder Contact. We will be using a Contact object as the placeholder for our selected Account in order to enable us to use an inputField to present this input as a lookup-type field.

Listing 7-3. Basic Controller Code for Account_Methods

```
public with sharing class account_Manager {

  //using Contact to hold selected Account
  //this allows the use of a lookup inputfield
  public Contact placeholderContact {get;set;}
  public list<Contact> accountContacts {get;set;}

  public account_Manager() {
    placeholderContact = new Contact();
    accountContacts = new list<Contact>();
  }
}
```

Tip   Do not forget to update your page with the controller attribute; remember Custom Controllers use the `controller` attribute rather than `standardController`.

Now that we have some accessible variables in our controller, we can update the Account_Manager page to actually have input and output data elements, as in Listing 7-4.

Listing 7-4. Account_Manager with Data Elements

```
<apex:page controller="Account_Manager" showHeader="true" sidebar="true"
tabStyle="Account">
  <apex:pageBlock title="Account">
    <apex:pageblocksection columns="1">
      <apex:inputfield value="{!placeholderContact.accountid}"/>
    </apex:pageblocksection>
  </apex:pageBlock>
  <apex:pageblock title="Account Contacts">
    <apex:pageBlockTable value="{!accountContacts}" var="c">
      <apex:column headerValue="First">
        <apex:outputfield value="{!c.firstname}"/>
      </apex:column>
      <apex:column headerValue="Last">
        <apex:outputfield value="{!c.lastname}"/>
      </apex:column>
      <apex:column headerValue="Phone">
        <apex:outputfield value="{!c.phone}"/>
      </apex:column>
      <apex:column headerValue="Email">
        <apex:outputfield value="{!c.email}"/>
      </apex:column>
    </apex:pageBlockTable>
  </apex:pageblock>
</apex:page>
```

This new version of the Account_Manager page in Listing 7-4 also contains some stylistic updates such as titles for the pageBlocks, the use of a pageBlockSection to arrange the Account section, and a tabStyle has been defined. There have also been columns specified for the Contact details once we load in an Account and have Contacts to populate it with.

You may have noticed in Figure 7-7 that when we were on the Account_Manager page, the tab that was selected in Salesforce was the Home tab. This is because, unlike with a standard controller, which defines a related object and object tab style, a Custom Controller could be associated with anything. We can specify that we want the page to

be primarily associated with Accounts by setting the tabStyle attribute to the value of Account, which is the object name. Now, whenever we are on the page, it will highlight the Accounts tab and apply typical page styling for an Account (the default is a darker blue color scheme).

Did you catch the error in Listing 7-4? All input elements must be contained within a form element. Currently, there is an inputfield element that is not within a form; if you try to save (if you haven't already), you will receive a warning informing you that the inputfield is not within a form. We can fix this problem by simply wrapping the Account pageblock into a form element as in Listing 7-5, and after saving, it should appear as in Figure 7-8.

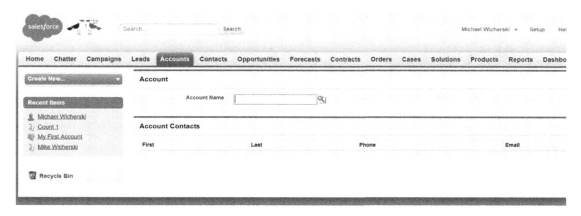

Figure 7-8. *Revised Account_Manager page with first input elements*

Listing 7-5. Account_Manager with First Form Element

```
<apex:page controller="Account_Manager" showHeader="true" sidebar="true"
tabStyle="Account">
  <apex:form>
    <apex:pageBlock title="Account">
      <apex:pageblocksection columns="1">
        <apex:inputfield value="{!placeholderContact.accountid}"/>
      </apex:pageblocksection>
    </apex:pageBlock>
  </apex:form>
```

```
<apex:pageblock title="Account Contacts">
  <apex:pageBlockTable value="{!accountContacts}" var="c">
    <apex:column headerValue="First">
      <apex:outputfield value="{!c.firstname}"/>
    </apex:column>
    <apex:column headerValue="Last">
      <apex:outputfield value="{!c.lastname}"/>
    </apex:column>
    <apex:column headerValue="Phone">
     <apex:outputfield value="{!c.phone}"/>
    </apex:column>
    <apex:column headerValue="Email">
      <apex:outputfield value="{!c.email}"/>
    </apex:column>
  </apex:pageBlockTable>
</apex:pageblock>
</apex:page>
```

You can already interact with this page! The lookup icon will allow the user to search for an Account record and select it, or to create a new Account (if your organization has quick create enabled—by default, it is). Unfortunately, we have not yet added in any functionality that would instruct the page as to what should happen when an Account is selected, so let us add that along with some other niceties, such as the ability to add a new Contact to the Account in Listing 7-6 and Listing 7-7.

Listing 7-6. Adding Account Load and New Contact Functionality to Account_Manager Class

```
public with sharing class account_Manager {

  //using Contact to hold selected Account
  //this allows the use of a lookup inputfield
  public Contact placeholderContact {get;set;}
  public list<Contact> accountContacts {get;set;}
```

```
public account_Manager() {
  placeholderContact = new Contact();
  accountContacts = new list<Contact>();
}

//select account by querying from placeholder value
//remember to select fields on contacts to display
public void selectAccount(){
  accountContacts = [select id,
                      firstname,
                      lastname,
                      phone,
                      email
                    from Contact
                    where accountId = :placeholderContact.accountId
                    order by firstname, lastname];
}

//reuse the placeholder Contact as our new Contact and save to database
public void saveNewContact(){
  insert placeholderContact;
}
}
```

Listing 7-7. Adding Account Load and New Contact Functionality to Account_
Manager Page

```
<apex:page controller="account_Manager" showHeader="true" sidebar="true"
tabStyle="Account">
  <apex:form >
    <apex:pageBlock title="Account">
      <apex:pageblocksection columns="1">
        <apex:inputfield value="{!placeholderContact.accountid}"/>
        <apex:pageblocksectionitem >
          <apex:outputlabel value=""/>
          <apex:commandButton value="Manage Contacts"
            action="{!selectAccount}"
```

```
        rerender="AccountContactsArea"/>
        <!--this rerender targets the Contact section by its id
          attribute and updates that section when a new Account is
          selected-->
    </apex:pageblocksectionitem>
  </apex:pageblocksection>
</apex:pageBlock>
<!--By using an outputpanel to wrap the entire Contacts area, we can
 control when it is Displayed and refresh, or rerender, only this
 section of the page-->
<apex:outputpanel id="AccountContactsArea">
  <!-- Use the rendered attribute to conditionally display elements;
    In this case, we only want to display Contacts if an Account is
    selected-->
  <apex:pageblock title="Account Contacts"
    rendered="{!placeholderContact.accountid != null}">
    <!-- Place button to save new contact at bottom of this block-->
    <apex:pageblockbuttons location="bottom">
      <apex:commandButton value="Save New Contact"
        action="{!saveNewContact}"/>
    </apex:pageblockbuttons>
    <apex:pageBlockTable value="{!accountContacts}" var="c">
      <apex:column headerValue="First">
        <apex:outputfield value="{!c.firstname}"/>
        <!-- You can use facets to control headers and footers of
          certain elements, here we are using the footer facet of
          columns to place elements into the footer of the table in each
          column-->
        <apex:facet name="footer">
          <apex:inputfield
            value="{!placeholderContact.firstname}"
            html-placeholder="First Name"/>
            <!-- html placeholders allow for clean looking suggestions
              that clear on input-->
```

```
          </apex:facet>
        </apex:column>
        <apex:column headerValue="Last">
          <apex:outputfield value="{!c.lastname}"/>
          <apex:facet name="footer">
            <apex:inputfield
              value="{!placeholderContact.lastname}"
              html-placeholder="Last Name"/>
          </apex:facet>
        </apex:column>
        <apex:column headerValue="Phone">
          <apex:outputfield value="{!c.phone}"/>
          <apex:facet name="footer">
            <apex:inputfield
              value="{!placeholderContact.phone}"
              html-placeholder="Phone #"/>
          </apex:facet>
        </apex:column>
        <apex:column headerValue="Email">
          <apex:outputfield value="{!c.email}"/>
          <apex:facet name="footer">
            <apex:inputfield
              value="{!placeholderContact.email}"
              html-placeholder="Email"/>
          </apex:facet>
        </apex:column>
      </apex:pageBlockTable>
    </apex:pageblock>
  </apex:outputpanel>
  </apex:form>
</apex:page>
```

Your page should now appear as in Figure 7-9. Selecting an Account and clicking Manage Contacts should now bring up a list of Contacts on the selected Account as in Figure 7-10 (our Contact from previous chapters shows up on the My First Account). Thanks to the rerender attribute on the Manage Contacts button targeting the Contacts

section, we can expand on the rendered condition of the Contacts section to only display the Contacts if an Account is selected, and update which Contacts are displayed when the Account changes.

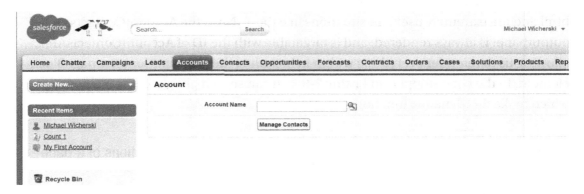

Figure 7-9. *Account_Manager with Account selection button and Contact save button*

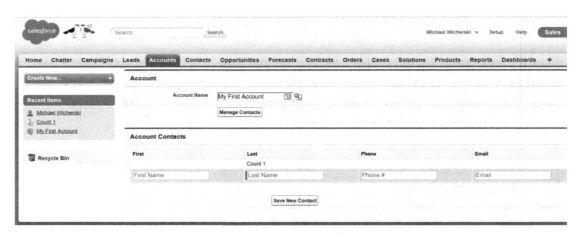

Figure 7-10. *My First Account selected and displaying the Contacts for that account*

Let us take a closer look at what is happening with the Contacts section, as this is a very powerful mechanism. The ability to selectively rerender portions of the page allows us to transcend static pages and instead create pages that react to the user's interaction, allowing us to create intelligent interfaces. Rerendering, or refreshing, portions of the page requires that the element you wish to rerender has an ID and is itself currently rendered, which means that our Account Contacts pageBlock would have previously violated that condition when an Account has not been selected yet. If the page loads with no Account selected, the Account Contacts pageBlock would never render, and

we would be unable to rerender it. It is important to understand that rerendering an element only rerenders elements within that element, not the element itself (this is why the element must already be rendered). It is therefore common to see elements wrapped into outputpanels. Outputpanels render as simple div elements when converted to html and are extremely useful in situations like these. Now, the AccountContactsArea outputpanel is always rendered, and is targetable with the ID of AccountContactsArea, allowing us to rerender everything within it, including the Account Contacts pageBlock element. In the code snippets in Listing 7-8, you can see a highlight of the elements which make this dynamic functionality possible.

Note   Rerendering is a powerful feature allowing only certain sections of a page to be rerendered, creating dynamic interfaces.

Listing 7-8. Rerender Functionality Code Highlights

```
...
<!--this rerender targets the Contact outputlanel by its id attribute and
  updates that section when the selectAccount action completes-->
<apex:commandButton value="Manage Contacts" action="{!selectAccount}"
        rerender="AccountContactsArea"/>
...
<!--this outputpanel wraps the Contacts section, is always rendered, and
  has a targettable id-->
<apex:outputpanel id="AccountContactsArea">
...
<!-- Use the rendered attribute to conditionally display elements; In this
  case, we only want to display Contacts if an Account is selected-->
<apex:pageblock title="Account Contacts" rendered="{!placeholderContact.
accountid != null}">
...
```

We are getting closer to having most of our basic functionality for this page in place. However, there is a bug, or at the very least undesired behavior, occurring on the

page right now. If you try to select a different Account (clicking the Manage Contacts button more than once), you are halted by a validation error on the new Contact's last name field (Figure 7-11). As the last name field is a database-required field, and it is being added to the Visualforce page using the inputfield component, the field-level validation is preventing us from submitting any action back to the server. This validation functionality is very useful in server-client applications, as it makes the application more efficient and faster by ensuring that data entry is valid before sending to the server. This cuts down on transmission time as well as processing since the client (the user's computer) will make sure everything is correct before submitting to the server for processing. However, in this particular case, we do not want this functionality when we try to select a different Account and we want to bypass this validation. We can accomplish this functionality by using an actionRegion within our form element. actionRegion is a special form control element which can be used within forms to group together pieces of the form to act together. In this scenario, we want to group the

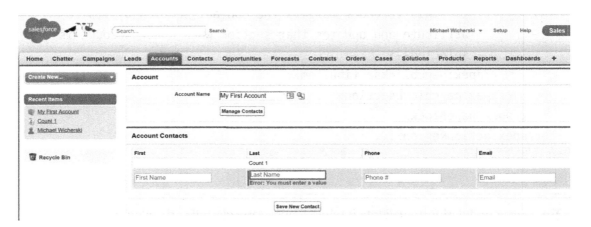

Figure 7-11. *Form validation error when trying to change selected Account*

Account selection lookup and button into an actionRegion. Doing so will allow us to execute that section of the form without considering the data in the remainder of the form, therefore allowing us to change the currently selected Account without error. The page code should now start as in Listing 7-9, with the entire Account pageBlock wrapped into an actionRegion.

Listing 7-9. Added actionRegion to Account Selection Form Section

```
<apex:page controller="account_Manager" showHeader="true" sidebar="true"
tabStyle="Account">
  <apex:form >
    <apex:actionRegion >
      <apex:pageBlock title="Account">
        <apex:pageblocksection columns="1">
          <apex:inputfield
            value="{!placeholderContact.accountid}"/>
          <apex:pageblocksectionitem >
            <apex:outputlabel value=""/>
            <apex:commandButton value="Manage Contacts"
              action="{!selectAccount}"
              rerender="AccountContactsArea"/>
              <!--this rerender targets the Contact section by its id
              attribute and updates that section when a new Account is
              selected-->
          </apex:pageblocksectionitem>
        </apex:pageblocksection>
      </apex:pageBlock>
    </apex:actionRegion>...
...
```

Tip   Be mindful of form validation when using <apex:inputField> elements.
Depending on the situation, workarounds may be necessary to achieve desired results.

The next step now is to verify that our Save Contact functionality works and that we are able to save new Contact records to the selected Account. At a minimum, we know we must enter in a last name; try to create a new Contact named Test Test2 by entering Test as the first name and Test2 as the last name and clicking Save New Contact. You should see that screen flash, indicating that the request was sent to the server, processed, and returned, after which the entire page was rerendered (the flash). You should also see that Test Test2 appeared in your Recent Items list in the sidebar. However, notice that Test Test2 does not show up in our Contact list for the selected Account as in Figure 7-12.

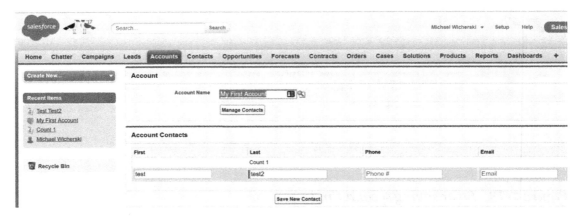

Figure 7-12. *Missing Contact after save*

If you had not noticed the Recent Items sidebar (perhaps the sidebar is hidden, or does not even render for the given page), your natural reaction would have been to hit save again. Try it, and you will get a nasty unhandled error like the one in Figure 7-13. The error indicates that we tried to insert a record, but also specified an ID. Since the insert operation is what creates the record and assigns it an ID, this is not allowed, and since our Contact had already been created we received the error. Both of our problems are due to the fact that we simply insert the placeholder Contact without doing any additional handling with respect to our page. Recall that the Account Contacts list is generated from the result of a query which is run only when an Account is selected. Inserting a new Contact for a given Account does not perform this query, which is why the Contact does not appear in our list of Contacts for the Account. Similarly, we did not reset our placeholder Contact after we inserted it with data we entered, and this is why we get the error when attempting to insert again. Both of these issues highlight the importance of being mindful of the fact that when we are creating custom pages with Custom Controllers, we really are recreating every little piece of functionality that is normally given to us by the standard controllers or standard UIs. See Listing 7-10 for how to handle both situations gracefully.

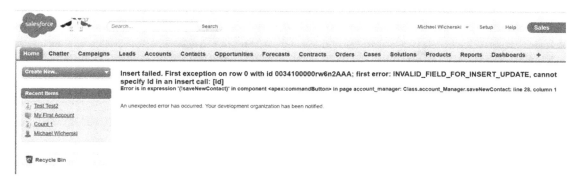

Figure 7-13. *Error saving second time*

Listing 7-10. Post Processing for Save Contact

```
public void saveNewContact(){
  //insert as a new Contact
  insert placeholderContact;

  //reset placeholder contact, but retain currently selected Account
  //when creating new sObjects, you can use constructor shorthand like this
  //to pass in variables to set fields and separating them with commas
  placeholderContact = new Contact(accountId = placeholderContact.accountid);

  //requery the Account contacts for selected Account
  accountContacts = [select id,
                      firstname,
                      lastname,
                      phone,
                      email
                   from Contact
                   where accountId = :placeholderContact.accountId
                   order by firstname, lastname];
}
```

This should now resolve all of our problems on the page, but our code is a little messy. We are now querying for the accountContacts twice, in two separate locations. This makes our code difficult to maintain. If a field is ever added to the table that we wish to query for, we would have to update the query in both places or we would encounter

errors. Remember that we are on a mission to make our code modular and reusable. We can achieve this by creating a new method called refreshContacts, which will be called by both our selectAccount and saveNewContact methods. The updated Account_Manager class can be seen in Listing 7-11.

Tip   Always strive to make your code reusable, grouping common actions into methods wherever possible. This ensures scalability and readability, as well as easy maintenance.

Listing 7-11. Updated Account_Manager.cls with refreshContacts Method

```
public with sharing class account_Manager {

  //using Contact to hold selected Account
  //this allows the use of a lookup inputfield
  public Contact placeholderContact {get;set;}
  public list<Contact> accountContacts {get;set;}

  public account_Manager() {
    placeholderContact = new Contact();
    accountContacts = new list<Contact>();
  }

  //select account by querying from placeholder value
  //remember to select fields on contacts to display
  public void selectAccount(){
    refreshContacts();
  }

  public void saveNewContact(){
    insert placeholderContact;
    //reset placeholder contact, but retain currently selected Account
    //when creating new sObjects, you can use constructor shorthand like this
    //to pass in variables to set fields and separating them with commas
    placeholderContact = new Contact(accountId = placeholderContact.accountid);
```

```
  //requery the Account contacts for selected Account
  refreshContacts();
}

//method to refresh selected Account Contact data
public void refreshContacts(){
  accountContacts = [select id,
                     firstname,
                     lastname,
                     phone,
                     email
                  from Contact
                  where accountId = :placeholderContact.accountId
                  order by firstname, lastname];
  }
}
```

When we reload the Account_Manager page and select our Account now, we should see that our Contact which threw the double save error before it did in fact save properly. You should also notice that our trigger from before is still active and has updated the first and last names of our contact to be property capitalized (Figure 7-14).

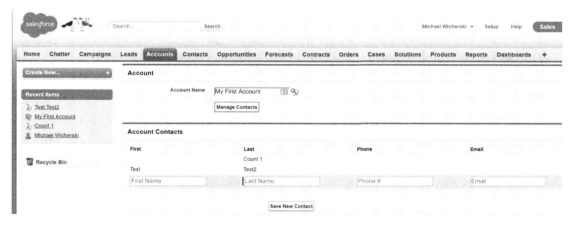

Figure 7-14. *Account selected with all Contacts with names formatted*

If we were to now create a new Contact, say My Test 3, and save, we should see the list of Contacts properly update with the newly entered Contact, but also that the placeholder Contact has been reset. As in Figure 7-15, the newly created Contact should also be sorted properly into the list of Contacts, according to our query which orders Contacts with `order by firstname, lastname`.

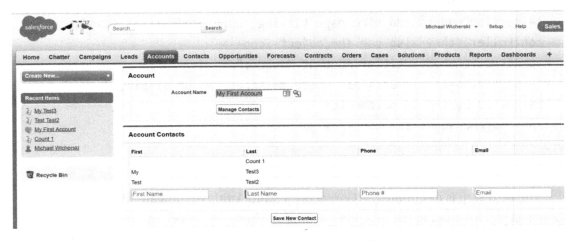

Figure 7-15. *Newly created Contact properly displayed*

Congratulations on building a fully functioning and useful for real-world application, custom Visualforce page and custom Apex Controller. This page is extremely barebones, but useful. It is now time to add some finishing touches to it to truly make it end-user-friendly. Consider the following situations:

- User wants to edit an existing Contact

- User wants to delete an existing Contact

- If user encounters an unexpected error, the error message is nasty as we saw before and crashes the page

- User is uncertain of whether or not their request has gone through and is being processed or has been completed

Some of these situations are easier to address than others, but do not worry, we will get to them all! Let us start by making the page a bit more user-friendly and indicative of where they are and what they are doing. As in Listing 7-12, let us add a sectionHeader

component to label our page, and update our pageBlock titles to be a bit more friendly, as well as add in a placeholder for our messages which will be displayed to the user.

Listing 7-12. Updated Page with Some Starting Elements for Display

```
<apex:page controller="account_Manager" showHeader="true" sidebar="true"
tabStyle="Account">
  <!--sectionHeaders add nice page titling; when used with a standard
   controller, they also use the object icon-->
  <apex:sectionHeader title="Account Manager"/>
  <!--pageMessages elements are where messages can be displayed; they are
   targetted by the id paramenter-->
  <apex:pageMessages id="messages"/>
...
...
```

The next step is to update the Contacts pageBlock title to indicate which Account's Contacts you are managing: imagine a scenario where you select an Account and click Manage. You then select another Account but forget to click Manage. Without this labeling, it is entirely possible that you are managing the Contacts for the wrong account! It is the little things in life... Listing 7-13 has the snippet to make you a superhero.

Listing 7-13. Updating the Contact pageBlock

```
...
<apex:outputpanel id="AccountContactsArea">
  <!-- load in Account details to indicate which Account's Contacts are
   being managed-->
  <apex:pageblock title="Account Contacts for {!placeholderContact.Account.
   name}"
    id="AccountContacts" rendered="{!placeholderContact.accountid != null}">
    <apex:pageblockbuttons location="bottom">
...
...
```

There is a small issue here, and if you were to try using the page now, you would get an error regarding the Account.name. It is currently null. We have to set the placeholder's Account (the entire record/object) value; currently, only the ID is set from selecting the Account via lookup. Since we need to set this value during both selection of the Account as well as when a new Contact is saved (remember we reset the placeholder Contact), it makes sense to update our refreshContacts method to perform this action as in Listing 7-14.

Listing 7-14. Updated refreshContacts Method to Also Set the Account Record on Placeholder Contact

```
//method to refresh selected Account Contact data
public void refreshContacts(){
  // we only need the Account name for now
  placeholderContact.Account = [select id,
                                       Name
                                  from Account
                                  where id = :placeholderContact.accountid];
  accountContacts = [select id,
                         firstname,
                         lastname,
                         phone,
                         email
                     from Contact
                     where accountId = :placeholderContact.accountId
                     order by firstname, lastname];
}
```

In Figure 7-16, we can now see our change to display which Account's data we are modifying. We can also see our added sectionHeader.

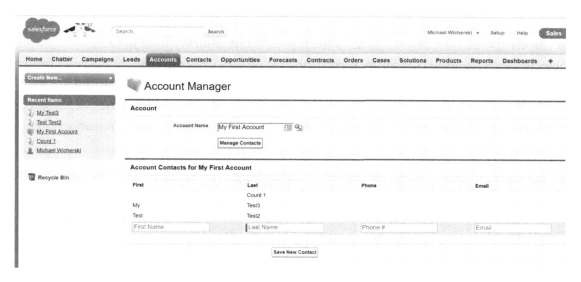

Figure 7-16. *Account data used to enhance user experience*

Continuing down the list of user experience enhancements, we can now add the ability to view and edit, as well as delete an existing Contact. Let us add a new column called "Actions" to the table with our Contacts and add links to View and Delete the Contact on that given row like in Listing 7-15.

Listing 7-15. Adding Actions for Contacts

```
...
<apex:pageBlockTable value="{!accountContacts}" var="c">
  <!-- actions for Contact -->
  <apex:column headerValue="Actions">
    <apex:actionRegion>
      <apex:outputLink target="_blank" value="/{!c.id}">View</
      apex:outputLink>
      <apex:outputtext value=" | "/>
      <apex:commandLink value="Del" action="{!deleteContact}"
        rerender="AccountContactsArea, messages">
        <apex:param name="actionContactId" value="{!c.id}"
          assignTo="{!actionContactId}"/>
      </apex:commandLink>
```

```
    </apex:actionRegion>
  </apex:column>
  <apex:column headerValue="First">
...
...
```

Notice that in Listing 7-15, the entirety of the Actions column is wrapped into an actionRegion. This is because of the deletion commandLink. This requires a server-side processed action, and, as our Manage Contacts button, would be halted by the placeholder Contact last name field being not filled in. A commandLink element functions like a button but presents itself as a link instead. The value attribute is the link text that is displayed, the action attribute is the method to execute, and rerender specifies which elements on this page to rerender on completion. Notice that messages are included as a rerender target for this link. We want to give the user feedback as to whether or not the Contact was successfully deleted or if an error was encountered.

The outputLink element allows us to generate a basic link. We could have just as easily used `<a href="/{!c.id}">View</a>`; however, in the interest of promoting Visualforce components, outputLink is preferred. The target attribute allows us to specify how the link is opened. By specifying _blank as the target, we are telling the browser to open this link in a new window (or tab, depending on browser). Not specifying this attribute, or setting it to _parent would have the effect of opening the link in the current window, navigating away from our manager page; this is undesirable, as you must then navigate back to the manager. The link we are navigating to, `/{!c.id}`, is simply the Contact's ID represented as a relative link. Recall that any record in Salesforce can be visited by going to the record's ID such as `https://na35.salesforce.com/0034100000rwSWu`. However, you should never hard-code your instance into a link. If your instance were to change, your link would no longer work. By using a relative link through /, you are instructing the browser to find the base URL, in this case, `https://na35.salesforce.com`, and append `/0034100000rwSWu` to it.

Caution   Never hard-code URLs into your pages or code—your application will break if your instance changes.

There is another new element being used in Listing 7-15 as well, the param element. This functions similarly to an inputfield in that it merges the value back to the variable in our controller or extension. However, it is only used with other

elements to add functionality to them. In this case, the param is adding functionality to our commandLink by passing the ID of the Contact which we wish to delete back to the controller before executing the deleteContact method. Although the name attribute on a param element is optional, it is best practice to include it, as this unlocks the functionality of retrieving page parameters (covered later) as well as increasing readability. The value attribute specifies what value to assign to the variable specified by the assignTo attribute. There should be a red flag going off in your head right now: we have neither a deleteContact method nor an actionContactId variable in our controller. Let us add those as in Listing 7-16.

Tip   Do not try to save your Account_Manager page before updating your Account_Manager.cls as in Listing 7-16; you will receive an error because the deleteContact and actionContactId variable do not exist.

Listing 7-16. Adding deleteContact Method and actionContactId Variable to Account_Manager.cls

```
...
/*although class variables can be placed anywhere in the class, it is best
to place them all at the top of the class. This variable is shown here
temporarily for illustrative purposes only*/
public string actionContactId {get;set;}

  public void deleteContact(){
    //perform the actual deletion.
    //All DML operations are exposed via the database class as methods
    //the delete method can take in an id or list of ids of records to delete
    /*here we are passing the id of the Contact assigned to the
    actionContactId variable*/
    database.delete(actionContactId);

    /*let us make use of the messages element to display a confirmation
    message on deletion*/
```

```
    //the syntax for this is quite long, see explanation in Chapter 7
    ApexPages.addMessage(
      new ApexPages.Message(
        ApexPages.Severity.CONFIRM,
        'Contact deleted successfully from account'
        +placeholderContact.account.name));

    //refresh the Contacts list to remove the deleted Contact
    refreshContacts();
  }
...
```

To test all of the new functionality, refresh the page. You should see the links for viewing and deleting Contacts after selecting an Account to manage which has Contacts. Try deleting one; you should see a confirmation message as in Figure 7-17. Notice that after you delete your Contact, in my case, the Count 1 Contact, it remains in your Recent Items sidebar list, but is no longer in your Contacts table. This is because we explicitly targeted the Contacts area when we rerendered—the sidebar did not get updated. If you were to try and click that link, it would take you to a page informing you that the record has been deleted. At this point, you should also test to ensure that your view links work to view the standard Contact view pages (and edit from there if need be).

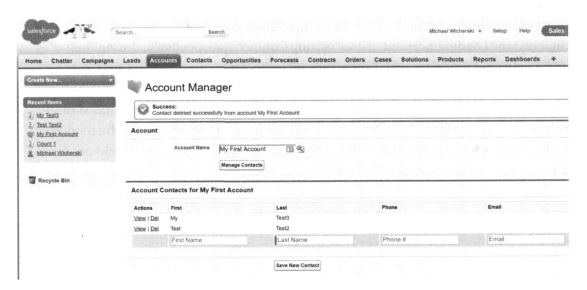

Figure 7-17. *Confirmation of new functionality to delete Contacts*

We also made explicit use of the pageMessages component by displaying a success message to the user. In order to add a message to the page, you must first construct the message and then add it to a special collection stored within ApexPages. The addMessage method on ApexPages will handle the addition for you, while the Message class constructor method will assist you in constructing a valid input to the addMessage method. The first parameter of the Message constructor is the severity of the message, which in turn is an Enum conveniently named severity. The three options for this Enum are Info, Confirm, and Error and are specified as ApexPages.Severity.Info, ApexPages.Severity.Confirm, and ApexPages.Severity.Error, respectively. Each is styled in its own fashion to reflect the severity; info is blue with an "i" icon, confirm is green with a checkmark, and error is red with an "x" icon. As you can see, constructing these messages each time is a fairly long process, but we will go over how to create a utility method to simplify this later in this chapter.

The final thing we want to do with our page is to add in feedback to the user and some error handling (more messages). Let us start by adding feedback for our users when they click buttons. There is a special component just for this called actionStatus, which allows for two different states: start and stop. Stop is the state your element is in when there is no processing occurring—this means both before and after an action. Start, on the other hand, begins its life cycle when an action begins, and ends its life returning to the Stop state, when the action completes. In other words, Stop is what you want your element to always look like, and Start is what you want it to change to while a processing action is occurring. We are going to disable both of our buttons and change their text to "Loading Account..." and "Saving Contact...", respectively, during their actions. For deletions, we will display a visual indicator of progress instead. See Listing 7-17 for snippets of the page on how to do this; altered code has been bolded to make it easier to follow. After these changes are made, your buttons and links should behave as seen in Figure 7-18. Note that code has been modified to force the rendering of these states for the purposes of demonstration in Figure 7-18—you should not have these states visible statically when you load the page.

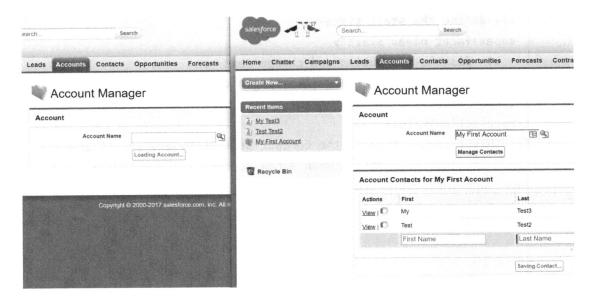

Figure 7-18. *actionStatus in the start state for each action element on Account_Manager*

Listing 7-17. Adding actionStatus to Buttons and Links

```
...
<apex:pageBlock title="Account">
  <apex:pageblocksection columns="1">
    <apex:inputfield value="{!placeholderContact.accountid}"/>
    <!--an id attribute is needed for the button to target for rerender-->
    <apex:pageblocksectionitem id="manageAccountSectionItem">
      <apex:outputlabel value=""/>
      <!--give the actionStatus an id to make it usable-->
      <apex:actionStatus id="manageAccountStatus">
        <!-- define the stop state-->
        <apex:facet name="stop">
        <!--define button as normal, add actionStatus to rerender targets
          and specify with the status attribute-->
          <apex:commandButton value="Manage Contacts"
            status="manageAccountStatus"
            action="{!selectAccount}"
            rerender="AccountContactsArea, manageAccountSectionItem"/>
        </apex:facet>
```

```
      <!--define the start state-->
      <apex:facet name="start">
        <!--disable the button and change text-->
        <apex:commandbutton value="Loading Account..." disabled="true"/>
      </apex:facet>
    </apex:actionStatus>
    <!--this rerender targets the Contact section by its id attribute
        and updates that section when a new Account is selected-->
  </apex:pageblocksectionitem>
 </apex:pageblocksection>
</apex:pageBlock>
...

...
  <apex:column headerValue="Actions">
    <apex:actionRegion>
      <apex:outputLink target="_blank" value="/{!c.id}">View</apex:outputLink>
      <apex:outputtext value=" | "/>
      <apex:actionStatus id="deletionStatus">
        <apex:facet name="stop">
          <!-- do not have to rerender the action column for action status to work
               as table is part of the contact area already rerendered-->
          <apex:commandLink value="Del"
            action="{!deleteContact}"
            status="deletionStatus"
            rerender="AccountContactsArea, messages">
            <apex:param name="actionContactId" value="{!c.id}"
              assignTo="{!actionContactId}"/>
          </apex:commandLink>
        </apex:facet>
        <apex:facet name="start">
          <!--standard spinner loading image provided by Salesforce-->
          <img src="/img/loading.gif"/>
        </apex:facet>
      </apex:actionStatus>
```

```
      </apex:actionRegion>
    </apex:column>
...
...
    <apex:pageblockbuttons location="bottom">
      <apex:actionStatus id="newContactSaveStatus">
        <apex:facet name="stop">
          <apex:commandButton value="Save New Contact"
            action="{!saveNewContact}"
            status="newContactSaveStatus"
            rerender="AccountContactsArea, messages"/>
        </apex:facet>
        <apex:facet name="start">
          <apex:commandButton value="Saving Contact..." disabled="true"/>
        </apex:facet>
      </apex:actionStatus>
    </apex:pageblockbuttons>
...
...
```

I have two questions for you. First, have you tried to click Save New Contact since we added pageMessages without filling in a last name? Second, have you ever tried to click Manage Contacts without selecting an Account? If you have not, try now. Otherwise, you should have seen that pageMessages automatically intercepted the error message from our inputField form validation, which is clear and understandable to the user, and that trying to manage an Account before selecting one throws a horrible-looking error message and crashes the page. As a developer, we should always strive to test our applications and make them as user-friendly as possible—but we will never be able to account for every interaction possible that our users may take. A major part of UAT is that once the developers believe an application is ready, they give it to the users, who inevitably find bugs and shortcomings, or come up with change requests. Nevertheless, we, the developers, should strive to make the experience as pleasant as possible, even when the user does something unexpected. We will be covering detailed error handling in the *Salesforce Developer Pro* title, but for now, we will add some blanket error handling that should get us by at a basic level.

Note   Form validation occurs before data is sent to the server for processing. This means that even if we add try-catch blocks in our controller, an inputField validation message will appear if relevant, since the request will never come to the controller for processing.

We can add basic error handling by wrapping every interaction into a try-catch block. A try-catch block is precisely what it sounds like: the code will try to execute, and then catch any exceptions which occur that would otherwise cause it to crash. The most basic form of a try-catch block can be seen in Listing 7-18, where a generic Exception is handled. There are specific types of Exceptions, allowing different error handling based on the type of Exception, which will be covered in the *Pro* title. Applying try-catch blocks with output messages to our Account_Manager class will result in Listing 7-19.

Listing 7-18. Basic Try-Catch

```
try{
  //code to execute
}
//catch the generic Exception type
catch(Exception e){
  // what to do if exception occurs
}
finally{
  /*an optional final step - this code will always execute whether
    or not an exception is handled.
  */
}
```

Listing 7-19. Updated Account_Manager Class with Try-Catch Blocks and Messages

```
//only relevant comments retained for clarity
public with sharing class account_Manager {

  public Contact placeholderContact {get;set;}
  public list<Contact> accountContacts {get;set;}
  public string actionContactId {get;set;}
```

```
public account_Manager() {
  placeholderContact = new Contact();
  accountContacts = new list<Contact>();
}

public void selectAccount(){
  try{
    refreshContacts();
  }
  catch(Exception e){
    //custom util method to add ApexPage.Message
    //getMessage method on Exception will provide the exception message
    util.addPageMessage('error', 'Error loading Account: '+e.getMessage());
  }
}

public void saveNewContact(){
  try{
    insert placeholderContact;
    placeholderContact = new Contact(accountId =
    placeholderContact.accountid);
    refreshContacts();
  }
  catch(Exception e){
    util.addPageMessage('error', 'Error saving new contact: '+e.getMessage());
  }
}

public void deleteContact(){
  try{
    database.delete(actionContactId);
    //updated to use custom util method for messages
    util.addPageMessage('confirm',
      'Contact deleted successfully from account'
      +placeholderContact.account.name ));
    refreshContacts();
  }
```

```
  catch(Exception e){
    util.addPageMessage('error', 'Error deleting contact: '+e.getMessage());
  }
}

public void refreshContacts(){
  placeholderContact.Account = [select id, Name
                                from Account
                                where id = :placeholderContact.accountid];
  accountContacts = [select id,firstname, lastname, phone, email
                     from Contact
                     where accountId = :placeholderContact.accountId
                     order by firstname, lastname];
}
}
```

In Listing 7-19, there is repeated use of a method in our custom util class called addPageMessage. The code for this method can be found in Listing 7-20, and it is simply a shorthand method for adding page messages by passing two parameters: a string name of the severity level and a message string. In order for the code in Listing 7-19 to save properly, you should add this method to your custom util class first.

Listing 7-20. Util Class Method addPageMessage

```
public static void addPageMessage(string severity, string message){
  //in case of capitalized input
  severity = severity.toLowerCase();
  //ternary operator to specify severity in constructor
  ApexPages.addMessage(new ApexPages.message(
    ((severity=='error')?ApexPages.Severity.ERROR:
    (severity=='info')?ApexPages.Severity.INFO:
    ApexPages.Severity.CONFIRM),
    message));
}
```

With our new try-catch blocks in place, trying to manage an Account before selecting one should no longer crash the page. Instead, a prettier error message should appear to the user as in Figure 7-19. Note that you must add messages to your rerender targets on

the Manage Contacts button if you have not done so already; otherwise, the page will simply rerender with no feedback at all. However, this error is still very cryptic to the user—after all, they most likely have not read this book to know what an sObject is. To say that this presentation of an error is OK is slightly cringeworthy, but the reality is that some errors will always appear this way until reported by a user. In this case, though, since we know this is a potential problem, we can safeguard against it either by requiring it via form validation or by handling this specific error explicitly in our controller. Although form validation (adding a `required="true"` attribute to the element) would normally be preferable, since that prevents a needless request to the server, in order to further demonstrate controller handling of errors, we will opt for that method in this case. The check is simple: in our `selectAccount` method, we simply check if the `placeholder.AccountId` is `null`, and if it is, display an elegant error message informing the user that they must first select an Account to manage. See Listing 7-21 and Figure 7-20 for this.

Figure 7-19. *Caught exception and page message outputting exception message*

Figure 7-20. *Handled known exception before occurence with custom message*

Listing 7-21. Handling a Known Error

```
public void selectAccount(){
  try{
    //check if an Account is selected
    if (placeholderContact.accountId == null){
    //inform user of how to correct
      util.addPageMessage('error', 'You must select an Account to manage
      first.');
      //exit method immediately
      return;
    }
    refreshContacts();
  }
  catch(Exception e){
    util.addPageMessage('error', 'Error loading Account: '+e.getMessage());
  }
}
```

Tip   You can use `return;` to exit out of a void method early. Void methods have no return, so specifying a return type, even `return null;` will not work.

At this point, Account_Manager is a fully functioning stand-alone custom page with Custom Controller, which is also very user-friendly. In the next section, we will make some modifications to load the page with a Standard Controller and our class as an extension to see what additional features that provides us with and how we can make this page even more versatile.

Standard Controller Extensions

In Chapter 4, we saw Standard Controller functionality and the ability it provided us to override the standard buttons for objects, specifically the new and edit buttons for the Contact object. Another feature that using a Standard Controller provides is the ability to embed your page on the page layouts of the object whose Standard Controller you are using. In the case of our Account_Manager page, it would be nice to allow users to make

use of the same functionality we have built out directly on a specific Account, without having to go to a special page and without selecting the Account.

With a relatively minor change to our controller class, we can turn it into an Extension instead. Extensions, like Custom Controllers, are Apex Classes which require a constructor. However, Extensions differ from Custom Controllers in that their constructor must take in a parameter of the ApexPages.StandardController type representing the Standard Controller they are extending. By adding the following constructor method in Listing 7-22, we can quickly turn our controller into an extension as well. Note, an Apex Class can be both a Custom Controller and an Extension, depending on which constructors it has and how it is utilized by the page calling it. Listing 7-23 shows the necessary changes to the Account_Manager page in order to utilize the Account Standard Controller and Account_Manager Custom Extension.

Listing 7-22. Adding Extension Constructor to Account_Manager.cls

```
//common abbreviation for the standard controller variable is scon
/*make sure this is a new constructor method, do not modify the existing
constructor*/
public Account_Manager(ApexPages.StandardController scon){
  /*just like in our custom controller, we need to initialize the
  accountContacts list*/
  accountContacts = new list<Contact>();

  /* we also need to initialize the placeholder Contact, but we already
  know the AccountId*/
  the Account Standard Controller will provide us with the id of the
  Account it is for*/
  placeholderContact = new Contact(accountId = scon.getId());

  /*this means that we can call the refreshContacts method right away,
  bypassing the
  Manage Contacts button click; but make sure there is an id first as best
  practice*/
  if (placeholderContact.accountId != null) refreshContacts();
}
```

Listing 7-23. Modifying Account_Manager.page to Use Standard Controller with Extension

```
<apex:page standardController="Account" extensions="account_Manager"
showHeader="true"
  sidebar="true">
```
...

Notice that the tabStyle attribute is no longer there and that the extensions attribute is plural. Since we are using a Standard Controller, the tab styling will be inherited from that object, so we no longer need to explicitly set the style to mimic the Account tab. As for extensions being plural, this is because the attribute can accept a comma-separated list of multiple classes to use as extensions. One important thing to note here is that if there is ever a conflict of variable names among the controller (using Custom Controllers with extensions is also possible) and extensions, the variable in the first extension wins. This means that if we have multiple extensions with a placeholderContact variable, the one in the first extension specified would always win with its values and state. It would also take precedence over any variable in the controller, if using a Custom Controller, called placeholderContact. We will explore this more in the *Salesforce Developer Pro* title.

Tip   Even with a Standard Controller specified, you can still use the page stand-alone (without specifying a record). The record provided by the Standard Controller is then simply a blank one, a new Account in the case of an Account Standard Controller, with no ID. Keep this in mind for future projects if the ID from a Standard Controller is a required value for the page to load properly.

In order to embed our newly embeddable page into the Account Page Layout,

1. Navigate to Setup

2. Navigate to Customize under Build

3. Navigate to Accounts

4. Select Page Layouts

5. Select the Page Layout to edit (there should be a default one named "Account Layout")

6. Scroll down in the "word bank" area to Visualforce Pages and select this option (Figure 7-21)

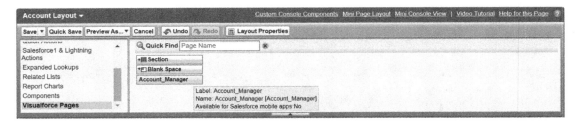

Figure 7-21. *"Word bank" on Page Layout edit screen*

7. Drag a new section from the "word bank" to your layout and call it "Contact Management", selecting the single column type (Figure 7-22)

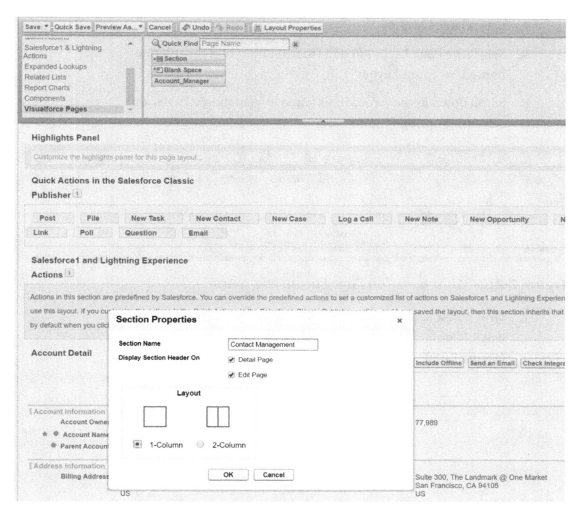

Figure 7-22. *Contact Management section creation*

8. Drag the Account_Manager Visualforce Page into your newly
    created section (Figure 7-23)

Figure 7-23. *Adding Account_Manager page to the Contact Manager section*

9. Save

If you go to an Account now (which uses the Account Page Layout), you will see your
page embedded there, with the Account preselected like Figure 7-24. Notice, however,
that there is a problem here. For one thing, if you click Manage Contacts, it looks like
nothing happens. This is not true; you simply cannot see enough of the embedded page.
To fix this, go back to editing the Page Layout and click the wrench icon on the blue area
that appears when you hover over the Account_Manager embedded page as seen in
Figure 7-23. This will open a window allowing you to specify options for the embedded
page, where you should set the height to 450 pixels and check the checkbox that is
labeled "Show scrollbars". In this way, you are ensuring enough space to use the page on
an average Account, while still allowing the user to scroll down if the page is longer on an
Account with many Contacts (Figure 7-25).

Figure 7-24. *Embedded page as visible on an Account record*

My First Account

Customize Page | Edit Layout | Printable View | Help for this Page

Show Feed   Click to add topics:

Contacts [2] | Opportunities [0] | Cases [0] | Open Activities [0] | Activity History [0] | Notes & Attachments [0] | Partners [0]

Account Detail   Edit   Delete   Include Offline

Account Owner	Michael Wicherski [Change]	Number of Contacts	2
Account Name	My First Account [View Hierarchy]		
Parent Account			
Billing Address		Shipping Address	
Customer Priority		SLA	
SLA Expiration Date		SLA Serial Number	
Number of Locations		Upsell Opportunity	
Active			
Created By	Michael Wicherski, 12/1/2016 3:00 AM	Last Modified By	Michael Wicherski, 7/24/2017 3:15 AM
Description			
Custom Links	Billing		

▼ Contact Manager

Account Manager

Account

Account Name   [My First Account]

Manage Contacts

Account Contacts for My First Account

Actions	First	Last	Phone	Email
View	Del	My	Test3		
View	Del	Test	Test2		
	First Name	Last Name	Phone #	Email

Save New Contact

Edit   Delete   Include Offline

Contacts   New Contact   Merge Contacts

Contacts Help

Action	Contact Name	Title	Email	Phone

Figure 7-25. *Increased height for embedded page on Account Page Layout*

There are several changes we can make using the dynamicity of Visualforce to make this page friendlier when embedded as well. For example, if this page is being loaded in the Standard Controller fashion, we can hide the header and remove the Account selection lookup altogether and load the page with only the Contact management portion. This would also allow the embedded page to take up much less space, which your users will be grateful for thanks to reduced scrolling. Look to Listing 7-24 and Listing 7-25 to see the changes made in bold.

Note   When specifying the height of an embedded page, you are "reserving" the space more so than specifying the actual height of the page. In essence, you are creating a frame. If the frame is too large, you will see whitespace, and if it is too small, you will have to scroll to see other pieces of the page. It is a very fine line of balance.

Listing 7-24. Account_Manager Class Optimization for Embedded Page

```
public with sharing class Account_Manager {

  //using Contact to hold selected Account
  //this allows the use of a lookup inputfield
  public Contact placeholderContact {get;set;}
  public list<Contact> accountContacts {get;set;}

  //variable to store Contact id for actions such as delete
  public string actionContactId {get;set;}

  //new variable to store whether page was loaded using Standard Controller
  public boolean usingStandardController {get;set;}

  public Account_Manager() {
    /*we know we are not using Standard Controller because this constructor
    was used*/
    //set control boolean to false
    usingStandardController = false;

    placeholderContact = new Contact();
    accountContacts = new list<Contact>();
  }

  public Account_Manager(ApexPages.StandardController scon){
    //we are using the Standard Controller because this constructor was used
    //set control boolean to true
    usingStandardController = true;
```

```
    /*just like in our custom controller, we need to initialize the
    accountContacts list*/
    accountContacts = new list<Contact>();

    /* we also need to initialize the placeholder Contact, but we already
    know the AccountId;
    the Account standard controller will provide us with the id of the
    Account it is for*/
    placeholderContact = new Contact(accountId = scon.getId());

    /*this means that we can call on the refreshContacts method right away,
    bypassing the Manage Contacts button click; but make sure there is an
    id first as best practice*/
    if (placeholderContact.accountId != null) refreshContacts();
  }
...
```

Listing 7-25. Account_Manager Page Optimization for Embedded Page

```
<!-- For readability, previous page comments were removed from this
snippet-->
<apex:page standardController="Account" extensions="Account_Manager"
  showHeader="true" sidebar="true">
  <!--using the control boolean to hide section header-->
  <apex:sectionHeader title="Account Manager"
    rendered="{!usingStandardController == false}"/>

  <apex:pageMessages id="messages"/>
  <apex:form >
    <!--hiding the entire form region for selecting an
      Account using control boolean -->
    <apex:actionRegion rendered="{!usingStandardController == false}">
...
  <!-- code snippet cut out -->
...
    </apex:actionRegion>
```

```
    <apex:outputpanel id="AccountContactsArea">
      <!--set the title ONLY if not using Standard Controller,
      set to blank string otherwise-->
<apex:pageblock
  title="{!IF(usingStandardController,'','Account Contacts for '
    +placeholderContact.Account.name)}"
  rendered="{!placeholderContact.accountid != null}">
...
```

After these changes have been made, your embedded page should look like Figure 7-26, and you can see how much space you have saved when comparing to Figure 7-25. The page should now fit comfortably within a 200-pixel-height window for approximately four contacts; a safe size would be 250 pixels to encompass larger Accounts and preserve some layout spacing. You now have a fully functioning Contact management page which can stand on its own, or be embedded on an Account Page Layout, and is optimized for both presentation modes. Remember that with great power comes great responsibility. If you provide pages like these, you will have to make sure that where you embed them makes sense to the users; in this case, you should probably hide the default Contacts related list from the Page Layouts where your management page is embedded to avoid confusion.

My First Account

Customize Page | Edit Layout | Printable View | Help for this Page

Show Feed   Click to add topics:

Contacts [2] | Opportunities [0] | Cases [0] | Open Activities [0] | Activity History [0] | Notes & Attachments [0] | Partners [0]

Account Detail

Edit   Delete   Include Offline

Account Owner	Michael Wicherski [Change]
Account Name	My First Account [View Hierarchy]
Parent Account	
Billing Address	
Customer Priority	
SLA Expiration Date	
Number of Locations	
Active	
Created By	Michael Wicherski, 12/1/2016 3:00 AM
Description	
Custom Links	Billing

Number of Contacts	2
Shipping Address	
SLA	
SLA Serial Number	
Upsell Opportunity	
Last Modified By	Michael Wicherski, 7/24/2017 3:15 AM

▼ **Contact Manager**

Actions	First	Last	Phone	Email
View	Del	My	Test3		
View	Del	Test	Test2		
	First Name	Last Name	Phone #	Email

Save New Contact

Edit   Delete   Include Offline

Contacts   New Contact   Merge Contacts   Contacts Help

Figure 7-26. *Reduced size of embedded page after optimization*

Tip Be mindful of how your embedded pages work with the rest of the elements on the page as determined by the page's layout. Keep your end user in mind.

Developer Guides and References

Throughout the chapters, especially those with Visualforce involvement, there have been times where attributes, parameters, or function definitions have been used without much explanation as to where they come from. Over time, you begin to memorize which elements have which attributes, and which classes/methods require what input. However, not even the most seasoned developer can remember all the options, and with three releases a year, there are bound to be a handful that are always new. For these situations, the pros and beginners alike can reference the Developer Guides released by Salesforce. They can be found at `https://developer.salesforce.com/docs`; the ones most relevant to this book are the Apex Developer Guide and Visualforce Developer Guide. There are also a few other documents here worth taking a look at:

- The Visualforce Workbook (although deprecated now, still contains valuable information)

- The Apex Workbook (also deprecated, but still useful for learning basics)

- Force.com SOQL and SOSL Reference

- Salesforce Developer Limits Quick Reference

The Visualforce Developer Guide is where you would look to find details about the Visualforce elements such as `<apex:pageBlock>` and what attributes are available for it. The Apex Developer Guide should be referenced when looking for more information about standard class functionality such as what properties are available for `ApexPages`, and what parameters any methods that exist there take; one such example would be referencing how to use the `String` method to check if a `String` variable is null or blank by using the method `String.isNotBlank()`.

JavaScript with Visualforce and Apex

Allow me to make a quick interjection here for any JavaScript developers out there, or aspiring JavaScript developers. If this does not sound like you, please skip this section, as learning JavaScript is outside the scope of this title.

Visualforce is fully capable of supporting vanilla (basic) JavaScript without anything special. Simply create a `<script>` element and off you go. The one thing to keep in mind is that if you want to select a specific element by ID, you must give every parent element

an ID, all the way to the `<apex:page>` element. Your ID selector for an element with two parents after the page element is then `pageId:parentId1:parentId2:elementId`.

You may also use JavaScript libraries such as jQuery or AngularJS 1 directly on the page by using a script import. Using other frameworks which require webpacks such as AngularJS (2 and 4; they have usurped the versionless name) is a tad more complicated but still possible. You would have to upload a Static Resource (under Develop in Setup) and then reference that Static Resource in your import statement(s). For details on how to do this, consult the Visualforce Developer Guide section on Referencing a Static Resource in Visualforce markup.

Tip   If you wish to use a webpack zip file, you can also host it externally at a publicly accessible location, which you can then import to your page.

Summary

This chapter has advanced quickly from a complete beginner to a developer capable of creating real-world applicable dynamic Visualforce pages with custom Apex Controllers and/or Extensions. Even with all the material presented here, we have only scratched the surface of the capabilities of Apex and the dynamicity of Visualforce. In the *Salesforce Developer Pro* title, we will dive in deeper to making the pages actually dynamically constructed with data in addition to having sections simply rendered based on conditions. We will also explore much more advanced Apex concepts around integrations and bulk processing in the *Pro* title.

In the short term however, let us focus on the next chapter. In Chapter 8, we will take a look at how to write test coverage for our existing Apex code in order to both fulfill the requirements to deploy our customizations to Production as well as verify that they are doing what we intend them to do. I would recommend you stop here for a little while and go back and review this chapter at least once. Perhaps try a different application of the same concepts in order to solidify your knowledge. A good challenge would be to create a page that would allow the user to add multiple Products to an Opportunity without leaving the page, as well as manage existing Products on a selected Opportunity in the same fashion as we enabled through the Account_Manager page throughout this chapter.

CHAPTER 8

Test Coverage and Deploying

Arguably the most important skill for Salesforce developers is to know how to migrate their customizations to a production environment. Recall from Chapters 1 and 2 that, although you can make changes to code directly in a Developer instance, in order to do so for a Production instance, you must first make your changes in a Sandbox and transition those changes to your Production instance. In this chapter, we will be taking a look at the predeployment checklist which must be completed in order to deploy as well as the tools which can be used for deployment.

Test Coverage

In order to deploy custom code to a production environment, Salesforce requires a minimum of 75% of your application code to be tested. What does this mean? Presumably (hopefully), you have already tested that your customization functions as intended before attempting to deploy. However, unless you wish to test the entirety of your application every time you make a small change, there needs to be some automated testing. This is where test coverage comes into play. In essence, test coverage is specific code written in order to execute your application code for the express purpose of verifying that your customization behaves the way it is intended to. Code designated as test coverage does not count against your organization's total lines of code limit, nor does it count against lines of code which must be covered by your test coverage. When we say that Salesforce requires 75% coverage, this means that at least 75% of your total lines of code must be executed by your test coverage.

The fact that test coverage is calculated based on total lines covered has bred a problem among newer and seasoned developers alike. Developers are more and more frequently starting to write test coverage which simply gets them line coverage rather

© Michael Wicherski 2017
M. Wicherski, *Beginning Salesforce Developer*, https://doi.org/10.1007/978-1-4842-3300-9_8

than testing functionality. Part of the reason is economical (clients do not want to pay for the time to write proper test coverage, which can sometimes take longer than the actual customization desired), while other factors include certain untestable features (certain things cannot be tested properly due to platform limitations, although this list is diminishing), lack of knowledge by the developer, and simple negligence or laziness on the part of the developer. In the following sections, we will take a look at both types of coverage and cover how to write proper tests.

Tip   Salesforce always recommends 100% test coverage. However, the required level of test coverage is 75% to deploy to a production server. Remember this if you plan on taking the developer certification exams.

"Bad" Test Coverage

What I refer to as "bad" test coverage is test coverage that is designed to simply run lines of code to get to the necessary 75% coverage for deployment, without actually verifying any functionality. For example, we have a trigger for the Contact object, which fires on beforeInsert, among other events. In order to deploy, Salesforce requires all triggers to have at least 1% coverage. The following code snippet in Listing 8-1 fulfills this requirement.

Listing 8-1. Bad Contact Trigger Coverage

```
//define a Test class
@isTest
private class TEST_Contact{
  // define a test method
  static testmethod void testContactInsert(){
    /* create a new Contact and insert it, triggering the before insert
    trigger event*/
    Contact c = new Contact(lastname='test');
    insert c;
  }
}
```

In Listing 8-1, a Contact record was created and inserted to the database. This will trigger the before insert event on Contact and fulfill the requirement of our Contact_ Trigger trigger being 1% covered. If we run this test (right-click the test class and run test from your favorite IDE), we will find out that we have 63% (19/30 lines) of contact_ Methods and 70% (7/10 lines) of contact_Trigger covered. However, what have we really tested? Recall that the beforeInsert trigger is calling a method which will capitalize the first letter of a Contact's first and last name on insert. The current test does not tell us whether or not this Contact's last name is now "Test" instead of "test". All it tells us is that beforeInsert and afterInsert events ran on the Contact (because this was an insert operation), and any chained event resulting from our application logic also ran.

"Good" Test Coverage

As opposed to the poor test in the preceding section, in this section we will add test validation to ensure that our application logic is performing as expected. "Good" test coverage is what a developer will need to know before attempting the level 2 developer certification exam from Salesforce. A significant portion of the score is centered around writing test coverage (in fact, it takes longer to write adequate test coverage for the solution than to implement the solution itself).

According to Salesforce, "good" test coverage will cover multiple use cases, including specific restrictions and error handling, as well as assert frequently that the application logic is performing as intended. Tests should also be run as mock users rather than only as a system administrator in order to verify access controls such as profile limitations and field level security. Compare the code from Listing 8-1 to Listing 8-2. AssertEquals is a system method that asserts that the first value provided (expected) is the same as the test value provided next (actual). In this case, we expect "First" to be the value of the Contact's first name. If it is not, an error will be thrown that reads: System. AssertException: Assertion Failed: Expected: First, Actual: first and the test will fail.

Listing 8-2. Good Contact Trigger Coverage

```
//define a Test class
@isTest
private class TEST_Contact{
  // define a test method
```

```
static testmethod void testContactInsert(){
  /* create a new Contact and insert it, triggering the before insert
  trigger event*/
  Contact c = new Contact(firstname='first', lastname='last');
  insert c;

  //retrieve the inserted contact
  Contact validationContact = [select id, firstname, lastname from
  Contact where id = :c.id];

  //verify the trigger worked to capitalize both first and last names
  System.assertEquals('First', validationContact.firstname);
  System.assertEquals('Last', validationContact.lastname);
  }
}
```

Test-Driven Development

In Test-Driven Development (TDD), the test cases and corresponding tests are written first, demonstrating that the developer knows the specific reasoning behind the logic to be developed as well as understands the specifications provided. Application logic is then written to fulfill those test cases successfully. In this development process, simple designs are preferred: allowing for a short development cycle, as all new application logic or altered existing application logic must only pass these new tests.

With regards to development in Salesforce, TDD has proven effective in stemming the writing of "bad" test coverage while also promoting more modular designs. The pitfall of TDD on the force.com platform is that it requires a great deal of planning, and it is very difficult to write code this way due to the inability to save the test to the server until the referenced code exists as well. A common workaround is to create the classes and method skeletons that the tests call for, save everything, and then flesh out the functions as needed to allow the tests to pass. Since tests are not run for Sandbox instances when changes are made, this design flow is acceptable.

Writing Tests

This section will be slightly more hands-on than the rest of the chapter as we dive into writing test coverage for our customization to date. Rather than explaining in theory what needs to be done, the test coverage code will be provided and explained through comments within the code. We will start with the contact_Trigger and contact_Methods classes (Listing 8-3), as those are database operations for the most part and therefore simpler. We will then progress on to testing our controller for Account_Manager, which will require us to mimic page visits and user interaction in order to get a good amount of coverage.

Test classes are just like any other class without a constructor. What distinguishes them is that they have an @isTest annotation before the class definition, and testmethod methods can now only be contained within test classes as of API version 27 (several years ago). Test methods should take no input parameters, and should never return anything. Since test classes have no constructors, test methods should also be declared as static, which also means that there is no way to control the order in which test methods execute.

Listing 8-3. Contact Methods Test Coverage

```
//define a Test class
@isTest
private class TEST_Contact{

  // test Contact inserting
  static testmethod void testContactInsert(){
    /* create a new Contact and insert it, triggering the before insert
    trigger event*/
    Contact c = new Contact(firstname='first', lastname='last');
    insert c;

    //retrieve the inserted contact
    Contact validationContact = queryContactWithNameFields(c.id);

    //verify the trigger worked to capitalize both first and last names
    System.assertEquals('First', validationContact.firstname);
    System.assertEquals('Last', validationContact.lastname);
  }
```

```
static testmethod void testContactUpdate(){
  Contact c = new Contact(firstname='first', lastname='last');
  insert c;

  //retrieve the inserted contact
  Contact validationContact = queryContactWithNameFields(c.id);

  //verify the current contact name is First Last
  System.assertEquals('First', validationContact.firstname);
  System.assertEquals('Last', validationContact.lastname);

  c.firstname = 'newfirst';
  c.lastname = 'newlast';
  update c;

  //requery validation contact
  validationContact = queryContactWithNameFields(c.id);

  //verify the update trigger worked to capitalize both first and last names
  System.assertEquals('Newfirst', validationContact.firstname);
  System.assertEquals('Newlast', validationContact.lastname);
}

//test contact counting on account
static testmethod void testAccountContactCounter(){
    //create a new account and insert
    Account acct = new Account(name='Test Account');
    insert acct;

    //validation account record variable for clarity
    Account validationAccount = queryAccountWithNumberOfContacts(acct.id);

    /*assert that there are no contacts counted for this account
    system.assert allows any condition to be validated, similar to an
    if statement*/
    System.assert(  validationAccount.Number_of_Contacts__c == null ||
                    validationAccount.Number_of_Contacts__c == 0);

    //create two contacts for account and insert
    Contact c1 = new Contact(lastName='last1', accountId = acct.id);
```

```
        Contact c2 = new Contact(lastName='last2', accountId = acct.id);

        //reduce number of dml statements by operating on a list collection
        insert new list<Contact>{c1,c2};

        //requery validation account
        validationAccount = queryAccountWithNumberOfContacts(acct.id);

        //assert account now counts two contact records
        System.assertEquals(2, validationAccount.Number_of_Contacts__c);

        //delete one of the contacts
        delete c2;

        //requery account for validation
        validationAccount = queryAccountWithNumberOfContacts(acct.id);

        //assert that account now only counts the one remaining contact
        System.assertEquals(1, validationAccount.Number_of_Contacts__c);

        c1.firstName = 'addingFirst';
        update c1;

        //requery account for validation
        validationAccount = queryAccountWithNumberOfContacts(acct.id);

        //assert that account still only counts the one contact
        System.assertEquals(1, validationAccount.Number_of_Contacts__c);
    }

    //test utility method to query contact with first and last names
    static Contact queryContactWithNameFields(id conid){
        return [select id, name, firstname, lastname from Contact where id
        = :conid];
    }

    //test utility method to query account with number of contacts field only
    static Account queryAccountWithNumberOfContacts(id acctid){
        return [select id, Number_of_Contacts__c from Account where id =
:acctid];
    }
}
```

The test class provided in Listing 8-3 will net you 100% coverage against both contact_Methods and contact_Trigger, and the tests assert the application logic functionality. In Listing 8-4, we will explore the necessary test methods to achieve coverage for the Account_Manager controller.

Listing 8-4. Account Manager Code Coverage

```
@isTest
private class TEST_AccountManager {

  @testSetup
  /*the testSetup method can be used to create test data which will can be
  used by test methods within this class and is reset once each method c
  ompletes, providing a clean copy for each method to  use simplying test
  data generation*/
  static void setup(){
    //create a default account with 1 contact
    Account defaultAccount = new Account(name = 'Test Account');
    insert defaultAccount;

    Contact contact1 = new Contact(lastname='lastname', accountid =
    defaultAccount.id);
    insert contact1;
  }

  //instantiate without standard controller
  static testmethod void AccountManagerStandAlone(){
    Account_Manager acctMan = new Account_Manager();

    //assert constructor initialized all default variables
    System.assertEquals(false, acctMan.usingStandardController);
    System.assertNotEquals(null, acctMan.placeholderContact);
    System.assertNotEquals(null, acctMan.accountContacts);
  }

  //instantiate with standard controller
  static testmethod void AccountManagerWithStandardController(){
```

```
//use the default account from  setup
Account defaultAccount = [select id, name from Account limit 1];

Account_Manager acctMan = new Account_Manager(
      new ApexPages.StandardController(defaultAccount));

//assert constructor initialized all default variables
System.assertEquals(true, acctMan.usingStandardController);
System.assertNotEquals(null, acctMan.placeholderContact);

/*assert placeholder contact set with account id from standard
controller*/
System.assertEquals(defaultAccount.id, acctMan.placeholderContact.
accountid);

//assert placeholder account variable updated with account data
System.assertEquals('Test Account', acctMan.placeholderContact.account.
name);

//assert account contacts have been initialized and queried
System.assertNotEquals(null, acctMan.accountContacts);
System.assertEquals(1, acctMan.accountContacts.size());
}

//instantiate without standard controller and test account selection
static testmethod void AccountManagerStandAlone_AccountSelection(){
  Account_Manager acctMan = new Account_Manager();

  //use default account
  Account defaultAccount = [select id, name from Account limit 1];

  //mimic user input to the lookup field on placeholder contact
  acctMan.placeholderContact.accountid = defaultAccount.id;
  //mimic the clicking of "Manage Contacts"
  acctMan.selectAccount();

  //assert that the account has been set and contact retrieved
  System.assertEquals(defaultAccount.id, acctMan.placeholderContact.
  account.id);
  //default account has 1 contact set in setup
```

```
        System.assertEquals(1, acctMan.accountContacts.size());
    }

    /*instantiate without standard controller and test account selection with
    error*/
    static testmethod void AccountManagerStandAlone_AccountSelectionError(){
        Account_Manager acctMan = new Account_Manager();
        //attempt to select without specifying account
        acctMan.selectAccount();

        //assert that an error message was presented to the user
        System.assertEquals(false, ApexPages.getMessages().isEmpty());
        boolean msgFound = false;
        for(Apexpages.Message msg : ApexPages.getMessages()){
            if (msg.getDetail() == ('You must select an Account to manage
            first.')){
              msgFound = true;
            }
        }
        System.assert(msgFound);

        //clear page messages
        ApexPages.getMessages().clear();

        /*mimic user input to the lookup field on placeholder contact
        account ids always start with 001, but specify an invalid id to throw
        error*/
        acctMan.placeholderContact.accountid = '001000asdfdas4esf4';

        //mimic the clicking of "Manage Contacts"
        acctMan.selectAccount();

        //assert that an error message was presented to the user
        System.assertEquals(false, ApexPages.getMessages().isEmpty());
        msgFound = false;
        for(Apexpages.Message msg : ApexPages.getMessages()){
            if (msg.getDetail().contains('Error loading Account:')){
              msgFound = true;
```

```
        }
    }
    System.assert(msgFound);
}

//test saving new contact, regardless of how account was selected
static testmethod void AccountManager_SaveContact(){
    //use the default account from  setup
    Account defaultAccount = [select id, name from Account limit 1];
    Account_Manager acctMan = new Account_Manager(
            new ApexPages.StandardController(defaultAccount));
    //mimic user entry
    acctMan.placeholderContact.firstname = 'first save';
    acctMan.placeholderContact.lastname = 'test save';
    acctMan.placeholderContact.phone = '2342342345';
    acctMan.placeholderContact.email = 'test@test.com';

    //mimic clicking save
    acctMan.saveNewContact();

    /*verify there are now 2 contacts displayed for the default account, 1
    from setup and 1 new*/
    System.assertEquals(2, acctMan.accountContacts.size());
}

//test saving new contact with error
static testmethod void AccountManager_SaveContactError(){
    //use the default account from  setup
    Account defaultAccount = [select id, name from Account limit 1];
    Account_Manager acctMan = new Account_Manager(
            new ApexPages.StandardController(defaultAccount));
    //mimic user entry, with error of omitting last name (a required field)
    acctMan.placeholderContact.firstname = 'first save';
    acctMan.placeholderContact.phone = '2342342345';
    acctMan.placeholderContact.email = 'test@test.com';

    //mimic clicking save
    acctMan.saveNewContact();
```

```
      //verify there is still only 1 contact
      System.assertEquals(1, acctMan.accountContacts.size());

      //verify error message was displayed to user
      System.assertEquals(false, ApexPages.getMessages().isEmpty());
      boolean msgFound = false;
      for(Apexpages.Message msg : ApexPages.getMessages()){
          if (msg.getDetail().contains('Error saving new contact:')){
            msgFound = true;
          }
      }
      System.assert(msgFound);
  }

  //delete default contact
  static testmethod void AccountManager_DeleteContact(){
    //use the default account from  setup
    Account defaultAccount = [select id, name from Account limit 1];
    Account_Manager acctMan = new Account_Manager(
          new ApexPages.StandardController(defaultAccount));

    //assert that default contact was loaded in
    System.assertEquals(1, acctMan.accountContacts.size());

    /*get the id of the first (and only) contact in the account contacts
    list collection*/
    id deletionId = acctMan.accountContacts[0].id;

    //mimic setting the action id by user clicking delete
    acctMan.actionContactId = deletionId;
    acctMan.deleteContact();

    //verify no contacts remain for default account
    System.assertEquals(true, acctMan.accountContacts.isEmpty());

    //verify confirmation message was displayed to user
    System.assertEquals(false, ApexPages.getMessages().isEmpty());
    boolean msgFound = false;
    for(Apexpages.Message msg : ApexPages.getMessages()){
```

```
      if (msg.getDetail().contains('Contact deleted successfully from
      account')){
        msgFound = true;
      }
  }
  System.assert(msgFound);
}

//delete contact error
static testmethod void AccountManager_DeleteContactError(){
  //use the default account from  setup
  Account defaultAccount = [select id, name from Account limit 1];
  Account_Manager acctMan = new Account_Manager(
        new ApexPages.StandardController(defaultAccount));

  //specify fake contact id; contact ids start with 003
  acctMan.actionContactId = '003000asdfdas4esf4';
  acctMan.deleteContact();

  //verify error message was displayed to user
  System.assertEquals(false, ApexPages.getMessages().isEmpty());
  boolean msgFound = false;
  for(Apexpages.Message msg : ApexPages.getMessages()){
      if (msg.getDetail().contains('Error deleting contact:')){
        msgFound = true;
      }
  }
  System.assert(msgFound);
}

/*mimic a standard user profile user accessing this page performing
actions*/
static testmethod void AccountManager_StandardUserFlow(){
  //locate the standard user profile
  Profile standardUserProfile = [SELECT Id FROM Profile WHERE
  Name='Standard User'];

  //instantiate a mock user with the standard user profile
```

241

```
User standardUser = new User(Alias = 'Std', Email='stdUsr@testorg.com',
  EmailEncodingKey='UTF-8', LastName='User', LanguageLocaleKey='en_US',
  LocaleSidKey='en_US', ProfileId = standardUserProfile.Id,
  TimeZoneSidKey='America/Los_Angeles',
  UserName='AccountManager_StandardUserFlow@testorg.com');

//run the test suite as the standard mock user
System.runAs(standardUser){
//use the default account from  setup
Account defaultAccount = [select id, name from Account limit 1];
Account_Manager acctMan = new Account_Manager(
      new ApexPages.StandardController(defaultAccount));
//verify standard controller initialized properly for standard user
System.assertEquals(true, acctMan.usingStandardController);
System.assertNotEquals(null, acctMan.placeholderContact);
System.assertEquals(defaultAccount.id, acctMan.placeholderContact.
accountid);
System.assertEquals('Test Account', acctMan.placeholderContact.
account.name);
System.assertNotEquals(null, acctMan.accountContacts);
System.assertEquals(1, acctMan.accountContacts.size());

//mimic new contact creation
acctMan.placeholderContact.firstname = 'first save';
acctMan.placeholderContact.lastname = 'test save';
acctMan.placeholderContact.phone = '2342342345';
acctMan.placeholderContact.email = 'test@test.com';
acctMan.saveNewContact();

//verify creation success
System.assertEquals(2, acctMan.accountContacts.size());

//clear page messages
ApexPages.getMessages().clear();

//verify deletion capability
acctMan.actionContactId = acctMan.accountContacts[1].id;
```

```
    acctMan.deleteContact();

    System.assertEquals(1, acctMan.accountContacts.size());
    System.assertEquals(false, ApexPages.getMessages().isEmpty());
    boolean msgFound = false;
    for(Apexpages.Message msg : ApexPages.getMessages()){
        if (msg.getDetail().contains('Contact deleted successfully from
        account')){
          msgFound = true;
        }
    }
    System.assert(msgFound);
  }
 }
}
```

You can see how writing test coverage for complex application logic can quickly get out of hand. The Account_Manager page is a fairly simple controller, and look at all the test coverage needed (Listing 8-4). Even the provided coverage does not meet all requirements of "proper" test coverage, but it is a happy medium between simple "line coverage" and full-out proper coverage, which would also include stress testing with mass data input for the triggers. When testing triggers, or any other "action" that could potentially impact a governor limit, it is also best practice to include the test segment containing the action into a separate test context block. This is typically done after all of the data is set up that is needed for the action, but before any asserts are done. In this way, the execution context of the test provides the most accurate representation of the application's logic impact on the server. See Listing 8-5 for an example.

Listing 8-5. Example Test Context Excerpt for Governor Limit Testing

```
static testmethod void testLimits(){
  //insert a test account
  Account testAccount = new Account(name = 'Test Account');
  insert testAccount;

  //create 200 contacts for the account
  list<Contact> contactList = new list<Contact>();
  for (integer i=0; i<200; i++){
```

```
  contactList.add(new Contact(lastname='test'+i, accountId = testAccount.
  id));
}

//initialize separate test context for limit tracking
Test.StartTest();
  //insert the contacts
  insert contactList;
Test.StopTest();

//query the account for verification
testAccount = [select id, Number_of_Contacts__c from Account where id =
:testAccount.id];

//assert the account has 200 contacts
System.assertEquals(200, testAccount.Number_of_Contacts__c);
}
```

In the example in Listing 8-5, the 200 contacts were inserted within a separate governor context. This means that although there were 201 dml rows committed in the entire test method (the account took 1 row), the governor limits were actually split into 1 dml row, and 200 dml rows within the start/stop block. This is useful when stress testing, because sometimes the setup data required uses up a large portion of the governor limit, either querying, performing dml, or simply execution time/script statements. The Limits class has methods which allow developers to track their usage against governor limits to ensure their code is efficient; this will be covered more in the *Pro* title in this series.

Deploying Customization

At last, we have arrived at the most exciting part of a developer's life: deploying changes into a live production environment. This moment is also the one that causes certain people to have anxiety attacks, and fairly often results in a cold sweat, increased blood pressure, and lost sleep—but the thrill is worth it!

Deployment Checklist

Luckily, the following checklist should help in preparing for that moment of truth—deployment—and make the endeavor one that gets celebrated rather than resulting in a gut-wrenching experience.

1. Write your test coverage. As explained in the preceding section, make sure your test coverage is good and covers multiple scenarios, and for different profiles.

2. Make sure you have at least 75% test coverage and that your triggers all have at least 1%, which is the bare minimum required for deployment.

3. Make sure your tests all pass. Run your tests, or run a "validate only" deployment (covered in the next sections).

4. Plan your deployment for a time when your user load is lower, your developers are available to troubleshoot, and hopefully you can have some guinea pigs, er... quality assurance testers, available. Monday evenings typically work well for this; planning for after hours or over the weekend is the best if possible.

5. Make sure to plan for a roll-back in case the features create problems and must be rolled back. Create a backup of anything you are updating or replacing if doing so.

6. Perform a data backup. This can be done either via a data loader program or via the Data Export feature under setup in Salesforce.

7. Perform a deployment validation well in advance of the planned deployment. This will alert you to any problems that you may need time to address before the deployment window.

8. Perform the deployment.

9. Validate functionality and user accessibility.

10. Celebrate.

Using IDE

Different IDEs have different processes for deploying changes, but it is typically called "Deploy to Server" or an obvious derivative of that. Most commonly, you will then be presented with a list of available files for deployment to select which items you wish to deploy.

MavensMate

Using Sublime Text 3 with MavensMate, you would select the MavensMate menu and then "Deploy to Server" as in Figure 8-1, which will present you with a prompt to complete the action.

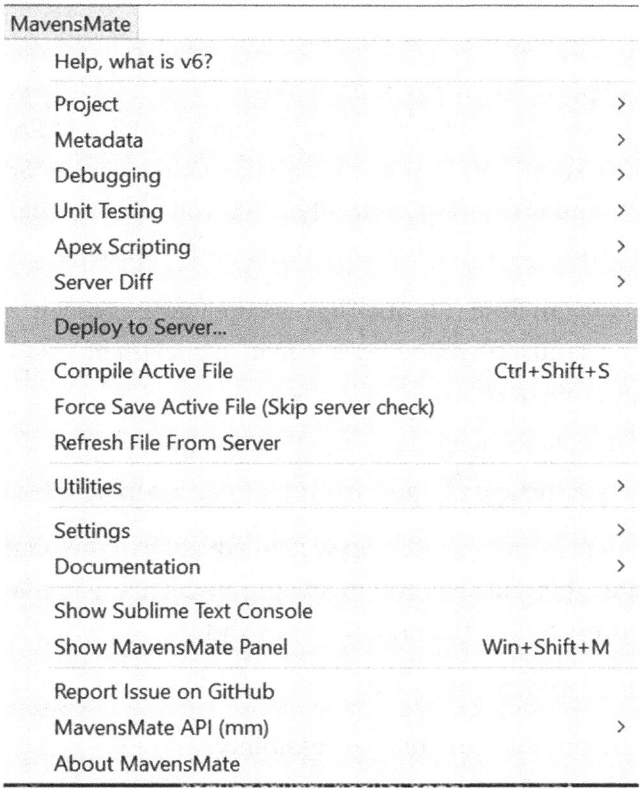

Figure 8-1. *Deploy to Server option in Sublime Text 3 with MavensMate*

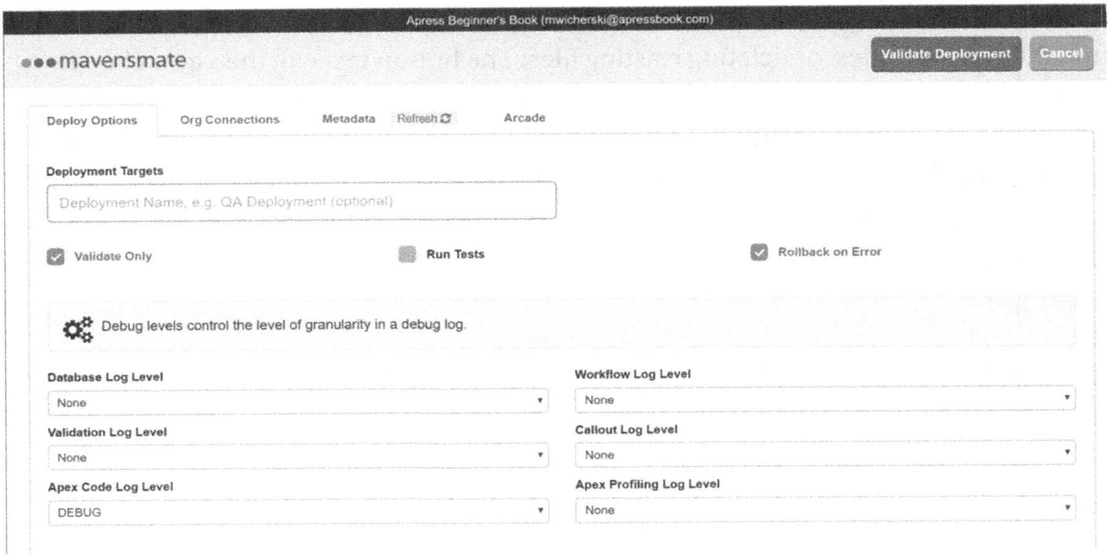

Figure 8-2. *Deployment prompt for MavensMate*

Note   The deployment prompts in the beta versions of MavensMate are slightly different, but the options are named similarly and the flow is the same.

You will notice in the MavensMate deployment prompt in Figure 8-2 that the primary button says "Validate Deployment". This is because the "Validate Only" checkbox is checked. A validation deployment is like a mock deployment. All necessary actions for a deployment are performed, but the changes are not committed. This is an excellent way to determine if there will be any issues with your deployment prior to your scheduled deployment window. Once you are ready to commit your deployment, simply uncheck the "Validate Only" checkbox.

The very first time you want to deploy using MavensMate, you must first create "Deployment Targets": the destination organizations to which you wish to deploy your changes. You can add deployment targets by switching over to the Org Connections tab and providing your credentials as in Figure 8-3. Once the connection is added, it will appear in the connections list on the right, as well as be automatically selected back on the "Deploy Options" tab. MavensMate will also remember your credentials and targets for you, expediting subsequent deployments to existing targets. The next step is to select which Metadata you wish to deploy on the corresponding tab as in Figure 8-4. The final step is to click "Deploy to Server". This will first compare your files against

the destination target, informing you of which action will be taken: creating new files, updating existing files, or deleting existing files. The button text will then also change to "Finish Deploy to Server". If you wish to complete the process, you must press the "Finish Deploy to Server" button and wait for the deployment to complete. Feel free to make use of the arcade while you wait. Once the deployment completes, a new tab will appear to the right of the "Arcade" tab, with debug logs regarding the deployment as well as a message informing you of success or failure, and in the case of a failure, what the errors were.

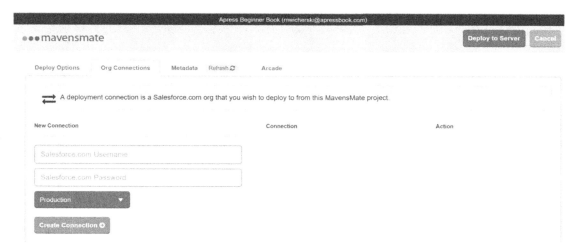

Figure 8-3. *Org connection tab in MavensMate deployment*

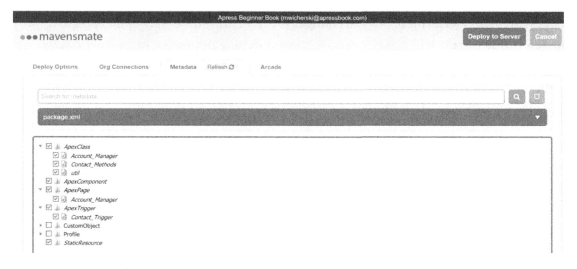

Figure 8-4. *Deployment metadata selection*

Eclipse

Deploying through Eclipse is slightly different. Whereas MavensMate allows for you to store your deployment targets and select from a complete list of your project metadata during a deployment, Eclipse requires credential entry every time. As for the metadata scope available for deployment, it is dictated by which directory you initiate the deployment from. In Eclipse, you can right-click any directory level within the project, including the project folder itself, and down to only a specific file. In Figure 8-5, the project itself has been selected to bring up the deployment prompt seen in Figure 8-6.

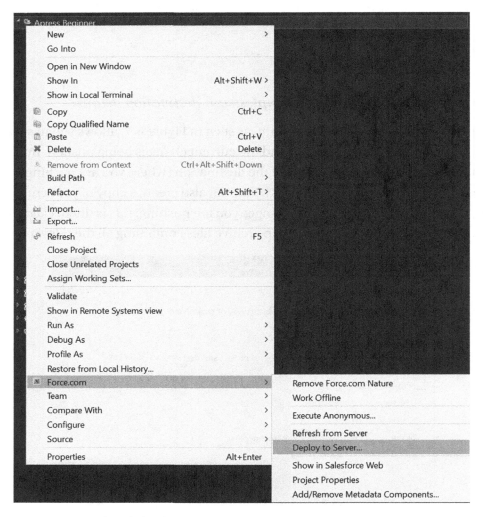

Figure 8-5. *Project-level deployment in Eclipse*

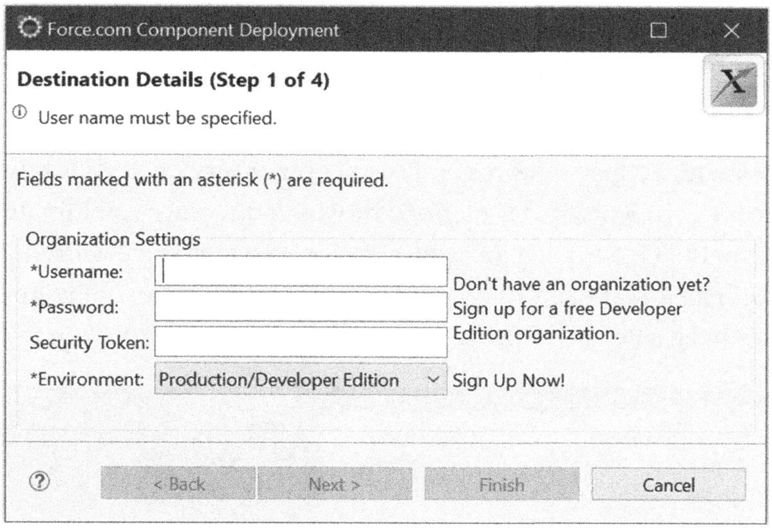

Figure 8-6. *Eclipse deployment prompt, step 1, destination details*

Step 2 of Eclipse's deployment prompt, as seen in Figure 8-7, allows you to save a copy of both the source being altered and the current changes being pushed. By default, it recommends that you create a copy of the destination (where you are pushing your changes to, in case you need to roll back). You can also create a copy of your current project, a snapshot if you will, of the changes you are pushing; this is unchecked by default. Both backups are provided as zip archive files containing all the relevant files.

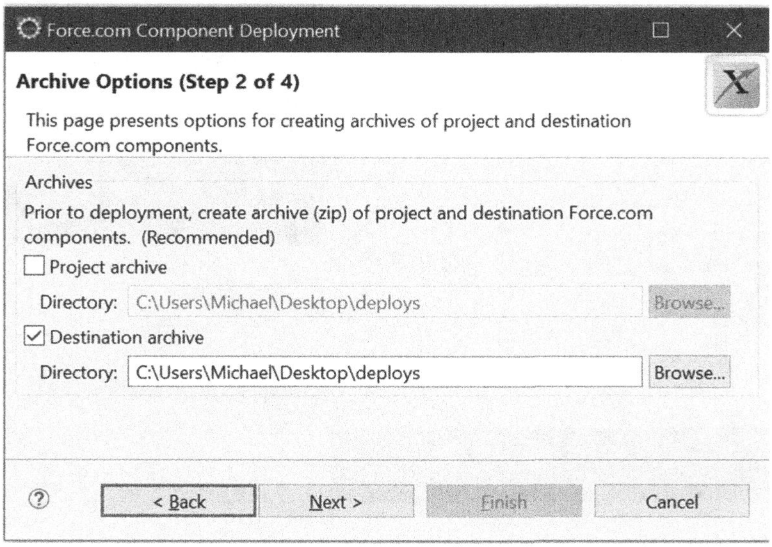

Figure 8-7. *Step 2 of Eclipse deployment flow*

In step 3 (Figure 8-8) of the Eclipse deployment flow, you will be presented with a list of metadata to deploy. Remember, this is determined by which directory you selected as your starting point; for example, if you had started the deployment from the Pages directory, you would only have Visualforce Pages available on this screen for deployment.

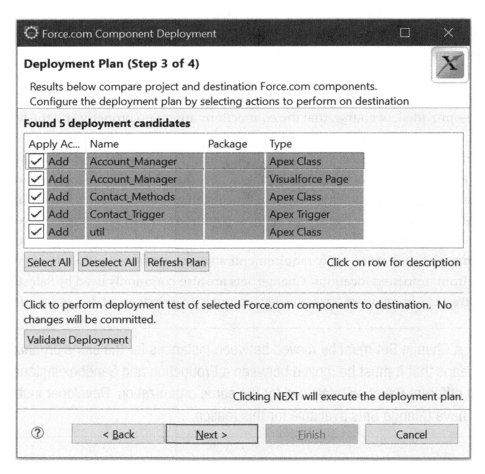

Figure 8-8. *Step 3 of Eclipse deployment flow*

Step 3 in the Eclipse deployment flow is also where you would opt to perform a validation deployment by clicking "Validate Deployment". Clicking Next on this step will actually execute the deployment, so be aware of the different operations. Step 4 is simply a confirmation screen which will present you with the deployment logs and a success or failure message with a list of errors if the deployment failed.

Using Change Sets

Another common way of deploying your changes to a live Production instance is via Change Sets. In order to perform a deployment using a Change Set, the instances must first be connected and enabled to allow Change Sets. In Chapter 2, we discussed how to enable Change Sets between the Production instance and Sandbox instance(s) for uni- and bidirectional Change Sets, so if you need to refresh your memory, go ahead and review that section.

Due to the nature of Change Sets, they must be moved between instances of the same organization. Production Change Sets can be deployed to any of the organization's sandboxes, and any sandbox can deploy to another sandbox or to the Production instance—provided, of course, that the connections are set up properly and the flow is allowed.

Change Sets are the slowest of all the deployment methods, as you must allow for time for the Change Set to upload, and then become available for deployment in the destination instance, in addition to the time it actually takes to run the tests (if applicable) and deploy the changes. The most common reasons for using Change Sets are to deploy metadata that is otherwise troublesome to deploy via an IDE, and to accommodate certain security requirements such as two-factor authentication or uploads from untrusted locations. Change Sets are also commonly used by Salesforce administrators who may not have any development experience and do not use an IDE.

Note   A Change Set must be moved between instances for the same organization. This means that it must be moved between a Production and Sandbox instance, or among different Sandbox instances for the same organization. Developer instances do not have Change Sets available for this reason.

Summary

At the end of the long and winding road of development comes the release of all that hard work into a live production environment. This chapter serves to cover that final step and its related processes to test and deploy customization. Although the deployment process is long, and Salesforce test coverage still has a long way to go before it is friendly,

it is up to developers to promote good test coverage and follow best practices in their deployments to ensure a smooth working environment for their respective Salesforce users.

Although this beginner's book has covered a vast amount of information, there is still so much more to the Salesforce world and capabilities of the platform to cover. The next chapter will outline where the journey of a new beginner Salesforce developer should continue.

CHAPTER 9

Path to Salesforce Developer Pro

All good things must come to an end. This is also true for *Beginning Salesforce Developer*. In this final chapter, we will take a quick glance at the topics covered in the next title in this series, *Salesforce Developer Pro*. Although you now possess enough knowledge to develop on the force.com platform, there is still a great wealth of information to be garnered and power to be harnessed from the platform, should you wish to continue your journey.

Governor Limits and Workarounds

Probably the most irritating aspect of the force.com platform is its shared tenancy architecture and related governor limits; ironically, this is the same aspect which makes it cost effective and as available as it is. We have already discussed governor limits at a high level throughout this book, but nothing we did really ran into any of them to cause concern. Nevertheless, as a Salesforce developer, you will undoubtedly run into issues with governor limits preventing you from executing that ever-so-awesome application logic you have created. While most of these issues can be overcome by using asynchronous processing, there are simply some things that cannot be done on the platform directly.

Asynchronous Processing

Synchronous processing is the regular flow of things wherein an action, either user interaction or database trigger, sets off a cascade of application logic. This logic runs in a single thread through to completion in a logical chain, and the entire chain must

© Michael Wicherski 2017
M. Wicherski, *Beginning Salesforce Developer*, https://doi.org/10.1007/978-1-4842-3300-9_9

complete in order for the action to be commited. In asynchronous processing, we are able to decouple certain actions to be processed at a later time so that the chain becomes smaller, and completes sooner, with fewer potential errors.

Asynchronous processing is best suited for logic which is not time sensitive or takes a long time to complete execution. An excellent example of this is our Account field, which counted the number of Contacts for that Account. Although it was nice to have that information available instantly, chances are that in a real-life scenario, the user could stand a delay of a few seconds or minutes to find out how many Contacts were attached to the Account. In such a scenario, we could move the entirety of that logic into an asynchronous thread rather than recalculate in the same thread as a Contact record operation. Asynchronous processes for trigger-related actions are best left to future methods, which are invocations of specific methods at a later time, or queueable classes.

Batch Processing

Batch processing is another form of asynchronous processing in which a certain set of actions is performed against a very large amount of data. The best use case for a batch class is one where a large amount of data needs to be processed either regularly, for example a nightly update, or even for one-off situations affecting thousands of records.

In batch processing, a data set is first derived for which the batch will operate, and then the batch performs a set of actions repeatedly on smaller chunks of the data set, specified as job size, which can range from a single record to 200 records at a time. Batch classes are defined as their own stand-alone classes and follow a very specific structure with required methods and constructors that must be included.

Interfacing with Other Services

For those situations where the force.com platform simply cannot perform what you need done, there are ways to interact with external services. The force.com platform is capable of both exposing your application logic as a service for an external system to utilize as well as connecting to an external service to perform actions on your behalf.

Using an External Service

Using an external service is an ideal solution for everyday tasks such as address verification, geocoding addresses, processing credit card payments, syncing calendars, syncing tasks, syncing contacts, and any other myriad of services available including actions such as posting to Facebook on your behalf or retrieving the number of comments a Facebook post has received. Any service providing an API can be utilized by you from the force.com platform.

Providing a Service

The force.com platform is also fully capable of taking your application logic and exposing it to the world as a service. This is an ideal solution if you need an external service to retrieve your data in a specific way. A great use case would be if a developer wishes to retrieve all of an Account's information, including all Contacts, in a single request. Normally, they would have to connect to the force.com data API and query first for the Account, and then again for the Contact information. Luckily, with this feature, you could whip up an Apex class and expose it as a service in just a few short lines, allowing that developer to make a single request to retrieve all the information together.

Dynamic and Smarter

We have only just begun looking at how Apex can dynamically adjust to a situation with our Account_Manager controller. If you take the time to plan it all out, Apex can be extremely versatile and dynamic, using dynamic Apex and dynamic Visualforce to code intelligent pages which can adapt to a variety of use cases. Beware, however, this brings with it difficult change management and scalability if done without careful planning.

Lightning

In the Winter 2016 release, Salesforce introduced the brand-new "Lightning Experience." It is a total refresh of the user interface and experience for out-of-the-box Salesforce. It also brought with it a brand-new development language and architecture. Unfortunately, as with all things new, it still has its problems to work out before becoming the de facto standard. For the time being, both technologies will reside in the Salesforce ecosystem.

Lightning Experience

The Lightning Experience is comprised of Lightning Components and the Lightning App Builder. The premise behind the entire system is that developers will create reusable components, which administrators can then use to build out applications as needed and tailor them to their specific organizational needs.

Lightning has the great advantage of being very JavaScript heavy, which has allowed for a huge influx of new developers who can work on the Salesforce platform, as the learning curve is much lower than having to learn Apex and Visualforce (assuming the developer already knows JavaScript). Salesforce's vision of creating a huge repository of components for administrators to use can certainly use the extra influx of developers and ideas, and all that is needed now is time for the components to be built and become available.

Lightning Design System

Along with the release of the Lightning Experience, Salesforce released the Lightning Design System (LDS). Although they both share the name Lightning, the LDS can be used as a stand-alone tool without Lightning enabled. In essence, the LDS is a compilation of all the styling that Salesforce uses in their Lightning Experience, which allows developers to quickly style their custom applications to match using whatever implementation language they prefer. If you are familiar with the concept of the Twitter Bootstrap library, this is something along those lines, but it is purely styling with no functionality, whereas Bootstrap does include some JavaScript functionality.

Summary

These are just a few of the topics that the *Salesforce Developer Pro* title will cover. With *Beginning Salesforce Developer* under your belt, you are well positioned to begin your career developing on the force.com platform, but the rest of this series will take you the rest of the way to really spreading your wings.

Hopefully, we will meet again in *Salesforce Developer Pro* to cover the topics mentioned in this chapter and more and again after that in *Practical Salesforce Development Projects,* which will guide you through several useful implementations from start to finish.

Index

A

Additive operator, 102
Apex programming language
    additive operator, 102
    arithmetic operations, 102–103
    break and continue, 116–117
    callout, 129
    classes, 118–119
    code development work, 8
    comments, 97
    composite data types (*see* Composite
        data types)
    constants, 101
    constructors, 120–121
    division operator, 102
    DML, 129
    do-while loop, 116
    flow control, 106
    for loops, 113–115
    function methods, 122
    governor limits, 128
    heapsize, 129
    if/else statements, 109–111
    large sample class, 130
    logical operators, 106–108
    methods, 119
    multiline comments, 97–98
    multiplication operator, 102
    OOP, 96
    primitive data types (*see* Primitive
        data types)
    queries, 129
    remainder operator, 102
    repetition controls, 113
    return methods, 119
    scope, 127
    script statements, 128
    sequential control, 108
    short circuit evaluation, 108
    single-line comments, 97
    statements, 96
    strongly typed, 95
    subtraction operator, 102
    switch-case statements, 111–112
    syntax, 96
    ternary statements, 112
    this keyword, 123
    thread, 127–128
    unary operations, 103
    variables, 98–99
    while loops, 115–116
Application Program
    Interface (API), 59–60
Arithmetic operations, 102

B

Batch processing, 256

C

Callout, 129

camelCase, 124

Cascading Style Sheets (CSS) language

    bold red font, 72

    cascading, 75

    embedded and external, 72

    inline, 72

    myClass, 73

    update embedded, 73, 75

Change sets, enabling, 20

Classes

    constructor methods, 137–138

    creation

        Developer Console, 133–134

        metadata file, 136

        modifiers, 134–135

        Salesforce, 135

    custom Apex controller, 144–145

    extensions, 145–146

    object class, 142–144

    utility class, 138–139, 141–142

Class methods, *see* Function methods

Composite data types

    collections

        Enum, 105–106

        list, 104

        maps, 105

        set, 104

    defined, 103

Compound assignments, 102–103

Compound data types, *see* Composite
    data types

Construct methods, 137–138

Constructors, 120–121

Conventions, coding

    camelCase, 124

    classes, 125

    constants, 126

    indentation, 126–127

    lower *vs.* upper camelCase, 125

    methods, 125

    names, 124

    variables, 125

convertToIntegerString method, 140

Custom Controllers

    Account_Manager

        account data, 202

        Account_Methods class, 179

        actionContactId variable, 204–205

        actionRegion, 193

        actionStatus, 207–209

        adding actions, 202–203

        adding new Contact, 188

        addMessage method, 206

        addPageMessage method, 212

        Apex Class, 176

        Apex Class creation, 177–178

        Apex Class edit screen, 178

        basic controller code, 184

        Contact pageBlock, 200

        Contact saving, post
          processing, 196

        data elements, 184–185

        deleteContact method, 204–205

        end-user-friendly, 199

        error handling, 206, 213–214

        exception message, 212–213

        first form element, 186–187

        formatted names, 198

        Info, Confirm, and Error, 205–206

        menu option, 180

        new Account_Manager page, 181

        new Contact creation, 199

        outputLink element, 203

Get the eBook for only $5!

Why limit yourself?

With most of our titles available in both PDF and ePUB format, you can access your content wherever and however you wish—on your PC, phone, tablet, or reader.

Since you've purchased this print book, we are happy to offer you the eBook for just $5.

To learn more, go to http://www.apress.com/companion or contact support@apress.com.

Apress®

Printed in the United States
By Bookmasters